D1372856

The
FULLNESS
of
PURPOSE

Taking Hold of Eternity Now

Dear Lyndsay

May God Bless
you with the
fullness of His
Purpose

[signature]

The
FULLNESS
of
PURPOSE

Taking Hold of Eternity Now

Ken Yasinski

One Way Publishing House
Saskatoon, Canada

The Fullness of Purpose
Taking Hold of Eternity Now

One Way Publishing House

©2010 Ken Yasinski

First printing 2010

ALL RIGHTS RESERVED

No part of this publication may be reproduced, stored in a retrieval system, or transmitted, in any form or by any means, electronic, mechanical, photocopying, recording, or otherwise, without the prior written permission of **One Way Publishing House.**

Published and Printed in Canada
ISBN: 978-0-9732075-8-3
Cover design and book layout: Adam Fahlman
Cover photo: Brian and James Toups
Printed by: Friesens (Manitoba, Canada)

Scripture quotations are taken from either
New Revised Standard Version Bible, copyright 1989, Division of Christian Education of the National Council of the Churches of Christ in the United States of America. Used by permission. All rights reserved.

or

New Revised Standard Version Bible: Catholic Edition, copyright 1989,1993, Division of Christian Education of the National Council of the Churches of Christ in the United States of America. Used by permission. All rights reserved.

Library and Archives Canada Cataloguing in Publication
Yasinski, Ken

The fullness of purpose : taking hold of eternity now / Ken Yasinski.

Includes bibliographical references.
ISBN 978-0-9732075-8-3

1. Future life--Catholic Church. 2. Holiness--Catholic Church. 3. Truth--Religious aspects--Christianity. I. Title.
BT913.Y28 2010   236'.21
C2010-906974-9

ONE WAY PUBLISHING HOUSE
Site 500 Box 17 R.R.5
Saskatoon, Saskatchewan, S7K 3J8
1-800-705-7396
www.onewaypublishinghouse.com

*I dedicate this book to
my beautiful wife Janelle.
Thank you for helping me become
who I have been created to be.*

Table of Contents

Chapter One

There Is More!

No eye has seen, nor ear heard,
nor the heart of man conceived,
what God has prepared for those who love him.
1 Corinthians 2:9

Purpose and potential, they go hand in hand. Lose one, lose the other. The *truth* behind why we are on this earth, our purpose, is needed in order to realize our potential. If we get the *truth* about our existence partly right, we will only experience part of our potential. The fullness of truth unlocks the fullness of potential.

We have one life to live and it is speeding by. I do not want to miss the complete picture of why I am here. Do you? To experience *the full potential* of our lives, we need to know *the fullness of truth* as to why we have been made.

God doesn't leave us to guess at the purpose of life. He doesn't bring us into existence and say, "Now figure out why I've created you." Somehow that doesn't seem loving. If you truly loved somebody, wouldn't you clearly communicate the most important things in life, especially when there are eternal consequences?

Wouldn't it be loving for God to give the people He has created a Church, free from error and deception, a Church that clearly points to the meaning and purpose of life, a body of teachings that His people could depend on to be true to eliminate confusion? The answer is "Yes," and He has. God has not left us standing alone.

The full purpose of our lives has been revealed in and through the Catholic Church because the fullness of truth subsists within her. This is the Church Jesus Christ instituted. This is the Church that Jesus promised the gates of Hell would not prevail against.[1] It is the Church He promised to stay with and guide through the power of the Holy Spirit. Our life finds the fullness of meaning when lived according to the fullness of truth, subsisting within the Catholic Church.

Keep Going ... Break the Lies

Some people may be thinking, "You're crazy, Ken. The Catholic faith is boring, impersonal, out-dated, unscriptural, stuck in man made tradition and not very attractive." I have heard these objections and many more. To those who may feel this way about the Catholic Church, could I challenge you with this: Is it possible that what you have come to believe about the Catholic Church is inaccurate? You might say, "No. I am a practicing Catholic," or "I was a practicing Catholic, and it was boring, not the purpose-filled life you claim."

If this was your experience, I am sorry that this is how it turned out. I am also positive that there would be nobody more grieved by this than your heavenly Father because you have not experienced what He intends for you to experience through the Catholic faith.

Very often we can form misconceptions about the Catholic faith which prevent us from finding and living the fullness of what God has for us. If we believe a lie, we will live our life according to that lie. If we believe that all there is to the Catholic faith is what we know or have previously experienced, we limit ourselves in the hands of God. We become unteachable. We may miss God's purpose for our lives.

A Boring Existence

I have a thirty gallon fish tank at home which *had* contained thirty-four tropical fish. I emphasis *had* because all that remains of the once vibrant school is a lone angelfish I've named Fuscles. His name is Fuscles because he's a fish with muscles. The guy just will not die. When I look at Fuscles, my angelfish, I think, "What a depressing life." All his friends died four years ago. He has nobody to talk to. He swims around and around in circles getting nowhere. And this is the kicker, he has been eating the same fish flakes for the last eight years. What a boring existence!

Could this be a simple image of our Catholic faith experience? We get up in the morning, go to work or school, do our routine and grind away for six days in the week. Sunday comes, we go to church, and then on Monday the routine begins all over again. Around and around in circles we go. And it feels like we've gotten nowhere. It is the same scenery every day. Faith is useless unless it is relevant.

Let's imagine that I get a new fish and put him in the aquarium with Fuscles who has his first conversation in four years. Their conversation goes something like this:

Fuscles asks this new fish, "Where are you from? I haven't seen you around here before."

The new fish responds, "I'm from the ocean."

"The ocean, what's that?" Fuscles asks.

"The ocean," replies the new fish, "is this big body of

water that has no beginning and no end. It goes all the way around the world. That is where I came from. That is what we fish are designed for. It gives meaning to our existence."

If you are the new fish and trying to explain to my Fuscles what the ocean is like compared to the experience of a thirty-gallon fish tank, it is impossible. The experience of an aquarium cannot begin to compare to the experience of the ocean.

Maybe St. Paul saw some of the Corinthians stuck in the tank when he reminded them of the scripture passage, "No eye has seen, no ear has heard, no mind has conceived what God has prepared for those who love him."[2] In other words, you will be blown away with what you will see and hear. Your mind can't even begin to imagine what God has in store for you if you love him.

God Offers Us a Relevant Faith

Do you really think that God would personally establish a Church that is useless to your life? Don't you think He has more important things to do than bore His people? The prayer of St. Francis reminds us that "it is in giving that we receive." If our faith ever gets boring, the problem is likely not God! He is infinitely creative. How much time do we *give* to nurturing our faith? How much attention are we *giving* to understanding the Church's teachings and why she teaches what she does? If we are not putting any effort into our faith life, then how can we expect it to be meaningful?

We have a relevant God, and He offers us a relevant faith. If this is not our experience, then we are not experiencing what He intends. Do you know why God has created you? The

Catholic Church has the answer. You'll just have to read the next chapter or the Catechism to find it out.

God's love is beyond all that we could possibly imagine. You can likely imagine some amazing things, but God is infinitely beyond them. If you have come to the point where you think you have all the answers concerning the Catholic faith and there is nothing left to experience, then you are in the fish tank. There is more!

There is more if you are just starting out in your faith walk. There is more if you have been a faithful Catholic for fifty years. There is more if you have just been confirmed or baptized. There is more if you have stopped practicing the faith, and there is more if you are Pope Benedict XVI. God is infinitely beyond all our knowledge and experience of Him up to this point in our lives.

❧

God is head over heels in love with us. He is longing to reveal this personally to our heart. Is it possible that we are in the fish tank and that there is a limitless ocean of Love waiting for us? With God there is always more. We must acknowledge this truth before our faith can grow deeper. If we don't, in the fish tank we stay.

Chapter Two

Created To Know God

God alone suffices.
St. Teresa of Avila

I grew up in a small, northern Saskatchewan town called St. Walburg. Within a forty-minute drive of our house there are many beautiful lakes to enjoy on a hot summer's day. One weekend our family and my uncle's family were out on a lake. The big deal was my uncle's new motorboat. Everyone was taking their turn either riding in the boat, skiing, knee boarding or tubing. There was also a more contemplative option for the less adventurous; it was taking a calm paddle in my dad's brand new canoe.

After awhile of taking turns between the motorboat and the canoe, one of my uncles decided it might be fun to switch things up. His idea was to pull the canoe behind the motorboat while he stood in the canoe and hung onto the ski rope. To our knowledge this hadn't been done before, but everyone agreed it was a great idea.

We jumped into the motorboat while my uncle stood balancing in the canoe, ski rope in hand. The excitement was building. My uncle secured his footing, leaned back, and gave the "I'm ready" nod. The motor roared; the canoe's nose lifted high in the air, and we were off. In a few short seconds we were going 20 km per hour, pulling the canoe with my uncle standing in the back hanging onto the rope: the birth of a new sport, "canoe skiing." We cheered my uncle on as he skimmed across the water faster than that canoe had ever gone before.

Our jubilation was cut short as he let go of the rope. We swung the motorboat around to give our congratulations. As we approached my uncle, still standing in the canoe, we noticed that he was now a little lower in the water than before. Something was not right. Pulling up to the side of the canoe we saw why. We had cracked the canoe in half! My uncle was sinking to the bottom of the lake.

Designed by God, for God

Knowing something's purpose is critical for realizing its potential. If you take an object and use it for something for which it was not designed, you have a good chance of breaking it and hurting yourself and others in the process. The purpose of my dad's canoe was to enjoy a quiet contemplative paddle on a lake. It was not meant to be pulled behind a motorboat at breakneck speeds. The result: we broke it. The reason: because we used it for something for which it wasn't designed.

To experience our life's potential we need to know the truth behind why we have been made. As with the canoe, if we live our life not in accordance to the truth of our design, we will hurt ourselves and those around us. Life will become empty and meaningless as we break up inside. Like the canoe pulled behind the motorboat, true happiness slips beneath the waters when we ignore our design. Unlock the full potential of your life. Know what God says about you through the Church He started.

So what is the purpose and potential of our lives? The Catholic Church is clear on this subject. The purpose of the life of man is to know and love God, and his potential is sainthood.[1] This is our design. This is our potential. God "calls man to seek him, to know him, to love him with all his strength."[2] When we set our sights on knowing and loving God, life takes on purpose, and we grow in our potential of sainthood. Anything that distracts or pulls us from God's invitation pulls us away from the purpose of our lives. When we are distracted from God, we get lost in this world. Knowing and loving God gives meaning to our existence. It is why we have been created.

Knowing somebody is much more than memorizing facts about them. Take, for example, Christopher Columbus. In the year fourteen hundred and ninety-two Columbus sailed the ocean blue. Likely you know about this event and about this person. Historically we know this happened and that Columbus existed. He is a significant person of history, but as important as Christopher Columbus is, we cannot know him. We can only know about him. You read the textbooks, and you get the facts. That's it. You cannot know him, because you cannot have personal contact with him.

Jesus of Nazareth was a man who lived two thousand years ago. This is also an historical fact. No serious historian would argue with it. Jesus was the son of Mary and Joseph. He was unjustly accused, condemned to death, and died on the cross. But unlike the case with Christopher Columbus, you can come to know the person of Jesus. You can come to know the person who lived two thousand years ago, and who still lives now. You can have a personal relationship with Jesus through the power of the Holy Spirit.

Jesus Christ is much more than facts, and you are much more than facts to Him. He gets excited about you. He is passionately in love with you. Jesus said, "I am the good shepherd; I know my own and my own know me."[3] Notice that Jesus didn't say He just knows about His own or that His own just know about Him. Jesus reveals that He is the shepherd and we, the sheep, can have a relationship with Him. Jesus says we can know Him.

Knowing Christ is the call of all people. This is one reason for baptism. In the words of Pope John Paul II, "It is necessary to awaken again in believers a full relationship with Christ, mankind's only Savior."[4] This relationship needs to be awakened again because some Catholics have fallen asleep or are unaware that Christ can be known.

St. Paul was a man who knew Christ. He lived as a Pharisee, the strictest sect of the Jewish religion,[5] but it was his personal encounter with Jesus Christ on his way to Damascus that changed his life. Paul proclaims:

> More than that, I regard everything as loss because of the surpassing value of knowing Christ Jesus my Lord. For his sake I have suffered the loss of all things, and I regard them as rubbish, in order that I may gain Christ.[6]

It is knowing Christ Jesus that Paul values above all else. In fact, all is trash, worthless to Paul, compared to his relationship with Jesus. Knowing Jesus is what gave purpose in his life.

To be Catholic and experience Christ personally should be the norm and should not be considered an exception. Pope John Paul II spoke of this reality. He said:

> Sometimes even Catholics have lost, or never had the chance to experience Christ personally; not as a mere "value," but as the living Lord, "the way, the truth and the life."[7]

We are created to be in a living relationship with Christ. We come to know Him as we begin to experience Him.

Relationship, Not Rules

For most of my teen years I thought being a good Catholic was about being a good person. I tried to be obedient to God so that I would go to heaven. I placed more emphasis on the rules of the Church than on the relationship with Christ which the Church offered me. As a result, going to church on Sunday and participating in the sacraments was very legalistic. It was something I had to do to please God.

Knowing God is not about simply acting "good." Our Catholic attitude is sometimes, "Follow the commandments; go to church on Sunday; be nice to people; act morally good, and you're a good Catholic." The problem with acting good is just that: *acting*. An actor pretends he is something he is not. Goodness comes from God's grace alone and not through our own efforts. Acting good, apart from grace, leaves us trying to earn heaven by focusing on our own works to justify ourselves. This way of life leaves us empty and frustrated. We reduce God to a boss for whom we work. When we're good, He rewards us. When we're bad, He gets mad and punishes us.

God the Father wants sons and daughters, not actors of empty legalistic works. He wants us to participate in His

Divine nature, not pretend it. He wants a relationship with us, to change our lives so that we can say with St. Paul, "it is no longer I that live but Christ that lives within me."[8] God wants to reveal His personal love to our hearts so that we might know and love Him.

When I was eighteen years old I attended a retreat that God used to change my life. I had heard of people being changed by God, but I thought those people were really messed up to begin with. I definitely wasn't one of those people. After all, I was a good person. I hadn't done anything really bad. I prayed once in a while. I went to church on Sunday. I acted the part of a good Catholic. I was sure of my "goodness," but I was also very conscious of an aching within me. I felt like I was missing something, but didn't know what.

As the retreat began, I noticed how into their faith some people were. They were singing songs like they meant it, speaking of Jesus with enthusiasm, and they kept talking about "the Lord." "It's good for them," I thought, "but there is more to life than religion."

In the evening of the second day of the retreat, something inside of me began to change. I found myself really listening to what the speaker was saying. His reflection on God's personal love stirred something within me. He talked of Jesus as if He were real, alive, and relevant. My heart began to burn, and I understood what I was missing. It wasn't rules my heart was longing for but a relationship with Jesus. I had been a "religious" person, but had never given the "reign" of my heart over to Christ to be my Lord.

Right in the middle of the talk I closed my eyes, and with a sincere desperation I asked Jesus to take control of my life. Through an act of faith, I chose to surrender. As I began to make this decision, I experienced the love of God. In that moment, Jesus became more real to me than I could have ever imagined. Tears began to stream down my face as I felt His tender acceptance. I knew that I was loved and that God had a plan for my life.

This experience left me changed. Jesus, now, was more than a guy in the sky. He was somebody whom I could know. I began to walk a path to rediscover my Catholic roots, but now things seemed different. I realized that I could grow in a personal relationship with God through participating in the life of the Church. The Catholic faith, I began to learn, was not about legalist rules and regulations. It points to the greatest love man has ever known: unconditional love.

Created to Rest in God

Did you ever wonder why God created man? What benefit are we to a supreme being who holds the universe in the palm of His hands? He is all powerful, all knowing and everywhere. He does not need us. He did not have to create us. There is nothing that we can do to add to His infinite glory. We are stubborn; we don't listen to Him; and at times we completely reject Him. Yet God went through the trouble of creating us. An examination of creation in Genesis may give us some answers.

On the first day, God said, "Let there be light," and there was light. And God saw that the light was good.[9] On the second day God created the Earth and sky and saw that it, too, was good. He continued to create on the third, fourth, and fifth days. On the sixth day God created man and gave to him everything He had created. Then God looked at all His hard work and saw that it was very good.[10] On the seventh day God rested. So what did man do on his first full day of existence? He rested with God.

If I were God, I would have created man on the first day and put him to work. Why not get man to share the load? I'm sure there was a lot to do! But God didn't do that. He created man and said to him, "Relax here with me, for everything I have is yours." God created man, not to work for Him, but to rest in Him. He created man, not to add to His glory, but to share His glory.

> God, infinitely perfect and blessed in himself, in
> a plan of sheer goodness freely created man to
> make him share in his own blessed life.[11]

Man was created out of love, to rest in God. Saint Augustine communicates this beautifully, "You have made us for yourself, and our heart is restless until it rests in you."[12]

Created to be Loved

Love is not just something God does, it is *who* He is.[13] If you are made to rest in God, you are made to rest in love. Love gives purpose and meaning to the heart, and if one does not receive love, devastating consequences can happen.

This is shown in the work of Rene Spitz, a psychologist who observed ninety-seven children in a South American orphanage, deprived of emotional or physical contact with others. Children, aged three months to three years, were not cared for adequately because of lacking of funding. Nurses fed, bathed, and changed diapers, but had little time to hold and cuddle the children as a mother would do. They tried to meet their basic physical needs, but the most basic need went unfulfilled: the need for love. Three months went by and many of the children began to show abnormalities. The majority began to suffer from loss of appetite, and they were unable to sleep. Many lay with empty expressions in their eyes. Serious deterioration began to set in after five months. With the withdrawal of their natural caregivers, many began to show symptoms of autistic children. They lay whimpering, with painful and haunted faces. Often, a doctor or nurse would pick up an infant only to have it scream in terror. Twenty-seven of the children died the first year, but not from lack of food or health care. They died from lack of love communicated through affective touch. Only twenty-one of the ninety-seven survived; most suffering serious psychological damage. [14] [15]

This example is extreme, but it points to the truth. We need love, and only God can satisfy this need. Without Him, our lives make no sense.

> Man cannot live without love. He remains a being that is incomprehensible for himself, his life is senseless, if love is not revealed to him, if he does not encounter love, if he does not experience it and make it his own, if he does not participate intimately in it.[16]

God desires that you participate in His love, but He needs your consent. Either you fight against God or you rest in Him. You fight against God by choosing your own ways instead of His ways. You fight against Him when you chose to live for self, instead of being Christ-centered. You fight against Him by leaning on your own understanding rather than looking to the wisdom of the Catholic Church. And when you fight against God, the heart gets tired. An aching begins to rise up that no amount of self-directed choices can satisfy. In the words of St. Thomas Aquinas, "God alone satisfies."[17]

No wonder restlessness results; you are up against the all-powerful God! Yet God allows you to win the fights. He allows you to choose your own understandings. And when you do, you are trying to rest in a place where rest does not exist. But God does not fight back. Instead, He opens His arms defenselessly on the cross, atoning for the fights you have picked with Him. The only place your heart will find rest, is in the arms that were stretched upon the cross for your salvation.

Jesus said, "No servant can serve two masters."[18] We are mastered either by God or by self: consumed by love or consumed by ego. We either serve God or serve self. One of them brings freedom, the other bondage. One brings rest, the other restlessness, but you cannot have both. Who is your master?

ود

Is Jesus just a person of history rather than your living Lord? Is your faith a burden? Are you doing all the right things but feel like a slave to God rather than His child? If your answer is yes, as mine would be at times, you have to start by making an act of faith, surrendering your life into the hands of God. We must acknowledge our need of Him before He can fulfill the needs of our heart.

This act of faith is not a quick fix. It simply begins us on the journey of our personal relationship with God. But it is absolutely necessary to grow in a purpose-filled life.

> Behold, I stand at the door and knock; if anyone hears My voice and opens the door, I will come in to him and will dine with him, and he with Me.[19]

Jesus is knocking on your heart. Have you answered the door?

Chapter Three

You Are Passionately Loved

*Whoever does not seek the cross of Christ
doesn't seek the glory of Christ.*
❧*St. John of the Cross*❧

On January 8, 1894, a little boy was born into a poor weaver's family near Lodz, Poland. His name was Raymond. He was full of passion and mischievous adventures, often testing the parenting skills of his mother. On one occasion after some mischief, his mother scolded him and her words finally got through to her son. A radical change of behavior resulted. Later Raymond explained:

> That night, I asked the Mother of God what was to become of me. Then she came to me holding two crowns, one white, the other red. She asked me if I was willing to accept either of these crowns. The white one meant that I should persevere in purity and the red that I should become a martyr. I said that I would accept them both.[1]

Raymond eventually was led to become a priest and in 1910 chose a new name – Maximilian Kolbe. By 1941, World War II had been raging for two years. Maximilian was arrested and deported to Auschwitz, the largest of the Nazi's concentration and extermination camps, where over one million innocent people were killed.

Upon arriving, the smell of death lingered in the air. The only way out, detainees were told, was through the smoke stacks of the crematorium.

One day the sirens sounded, indicating that there had been an escape. A roll call of Maximilian's cell block revealed one person missing. In reprisal, the Nazi guard in command ordered ten people to be randomly selected from the cell block. These men were to be sent to an underground starvation bunker to die. This was to serve as punishment for those who had escaped and to deter others with such plans.

As the Nazis began to select their ten victims, one man chosen, Franciszek Gajowniczek, began to cry, "My wife! My children! I will never see them again!"

When he uttered this cry of dismay, Maximilian stepped silently forward, took off his cap, stood before the commandant and said, "I am a Catholic priest. Let me take his place. I am old. He has a wife and children."

Astounded, the Nazi commandant asked, "What does this Polish pig want?"

Kolbe pointed with his hand to the condemned Franciszek Gajowniczek and repeated. "I am a Catholic priest from Poland; I would like to take his place, because he has a wife and children."[2]

After some thought, the guard accepted the offer, and Maximilian joined the line of the doomed.

Gajowniczek later recalled:

> I could only thank him with my eyes. I was stunned and could hardly grasp what was going on. The immensity of it: I, the condemned, am to live and someone else willingly and voluntari-

ly offers his life for me - a stranger. Is this some dream?[3]

Maximilian was thrown down the stairs into the starvation bunker with the rest of the group. Hunger began to gnaw away at their stomachs, and some began to lick the condensation on the stones, hoping to catch some moisture. The whole time, Kolbe encouraged the group. He taught them to sing the psalms, pray, and mediate on the passion of Christ. After two weeks, only four were alive; Maximilian, the only conscious one. The cell was now needed for more victims. The Nazis couldn't wait any longer for them to die. A guard came to inject a lethal dose of carbolic acid into the left arm of each man. Kolbe, the last to be injected, lifted up his arm. He died on August 14, 1941.

Maximilian offered his life for the freedom of another. What moved him to such heroic virtue? As Blessed Mother Teresa of Calcutta would put it, *"Love transforms one into what one loves."* Kolbe loved Jesus and knew the freedom won through the cross. He possessed the love of Christ and was transformed into His image. He embodied the love of Jesus and gave his life for another. St. Maximilian Kolbe was a purpose-driven Catholic.

To be transformed into the image of Jesus, one must receive His love. It is difficult to do this if one knows little of Jesus and what He has done. Do you know what His love looks like? Look at the crucifix and you will see love in action. Upon the cross is the mystery of God's love for you. If you desire to know God's love more deeply, mediate on the passion. There you will encounter His passionate love.

The passion of Jesus reveals His passionate love for you.

It reveals His perfect obedience to God the Father and His perfect love for you. The Church teaches that Jesus knew and loved you personally when He offered His life.[4] You were continuously present to Jesus in a mysterious way throughout His life, passion, death, and resurrection. You had no consciousness of Jesus 2000 years ago, but He was very aware of you, since it was for your sake He offered His life. He knew your every thought, motive, and action. He saw all, even the deepest, darkest secrets of the heart. And yet, He loved all.

All that Jesus did during His life was an expression of love for you. Each word of Jesus recorded in the Gospels had you in mind. His miracles, actions, and way of life are all a revelation of Divine love. Jesus' passion is no exception. It is His sacrifice of love, endured for you.

From Bad to Worse

Picture Jesus in the garden of Gethsemane. He is experiencing unimaginable agony. Jesus knows that His passion is beginning. The consequence of man's sin is upon Him. Death is right around the corner. His heart is racing, body sweating, and He is sorrowful to the point of death.[5] In the midst of this darkness He cries out to God, "Father, if you are willing, remove this cup from me; yet, not my will but yours be done."[6] An angel comforts Him, but Jesus' agony only increases after He prays, and His sweat becomes drops of blood.[7]

The sweating of blood can be misunderstood as an exaggeration in the Bible. This is not so. It is a rare condition called hematidrosis, associated with fear. It can happen when the body suffers extreme tension and anxiety, causing the capillaries in the sweat glands to rupture, resulting in blood-stained sweat.[8]

Jesus prays, and His suffering increases! Jesus embraces this suffering and remains faithful to the will of God the Father. He embraces this suffering because He embraces the consequences of sin. He accepts the duty to carry our sins in His body, "becoming obedient unto death."[9]

Have you ever prayed, and it seems things have gotten worse? Jesus knows what that is like and had you in mind in the garden.

Jesus picks Himself off the ground where He was praying and sees His Apostles fast asleep.[10] He wakes them up in the midst of confusion as His betrayer, Judas, comes forward to kiss Him. Jesus turns to Judas and looks into his eyes. His heart must have been grieved, yet He says to him, "Friend, do what you are here to do."[11]

I've always considered Judas a betrayer, the one who sold out Christ. But Jesus calls him friend! I could have thought of many other things to call him. Friend would not have been in my vocabulary. But Jesus' love is never exhausted. Judas has sold out Jesus for thirty pieces of silver, and yet Jesus calls him to friendship.

The love of Jesus goes beyond all betrayal, no matter how big. The fact is, all of us have betrayed Christ, yet Jesus turns to each of us and calls us friend!

The soldiers then seize Jesus. Peter pulls out a sword to protect his Lord, cutting off the ear of the high priest's slave.[12] Do you think Peter was aiming for the ear? I don't think so! Peter was going for the neck and missed. It turns out that Peter was better with a fishing rod than with a sword.

What Jesus says next is amazing. "Do you think that I

cannot appeal to my Father, and he will at once send me more than twelve legions of angels?"[13] One legion of troops in the Roman army was six thousand men. In other words, Jesus is saying, "Peter, don't you know that if I asked my Father, He would send seventy-two thousand angels!" Jesus knows that He can ask for help. He knows there is a way out, but He also knows you. He chose the passion when He chose you. You are passionately loved.

We Are Each the Author of Christ's Passion

Jesus' passion continues. His best friends abandon Him; He is falsely accused, and nobody comes to His defense. Then Jesus hears the rooster crow and knows Peter has denied him. All this must have pained His heart immensely. Add to this the weight of sin for every time you have denied and abandoned Christ. Add again the weight of sin for every time man throughout history has not responded to the grace of God.[14] This was the cross Jesus carried, even before it was placed upon His shoulders. "Sinners were the authors and the ministers of all the sufferings that the divine Redeemer endured."[15]

"Pilate then took Jesus and scourged Him."[16] This is a short, simple verse in John 19:1, and if read quickly, it could be missed or forgotten. Jesus was scourged. No description, just the fact. It is likely no great detail is given because the early readers of the Gospels would have fully understood the horrific nature of scourging. We, on the other hand, do not.

The Shroud of Turin is thought by many to be the actual burial cloth of Jesus. It reveals, in great detail, the type of beating Jesus received. The Roman whip was made up of two or three leather thongs at the ends, on which were tied small bits of either bone or metal.[17] The whip would have been used to inflict a great deal of pain, breaking the skin. The Shroud reveals between one hundred to one hundred and twenty whip marks that covered the shoulders, lower back, buttock, and calves of Jesus. The force of the blows would have been enough to break a rib or collapse a lung. And to think that at any time Jesus could have asked for seventy-two thousand angels for help!

> But he was wounded for our transgressions, he was bruised for our iniquities; upon him was the chastisement that made us whole, and with his *stripes* we are healed [emphasis added].[18]

Love Proves Itself with Sacrifice

Three times Jesus falls. Dehydrated and weakened from His scourging, He is unable to carry the physical weight of the cross. Jesus' exposed knees scrape against the rocks on the road while the weight of the cross smashes His body to the ground.

By the third fall Jesus is near death, and the soldiers know it. Why else would they have forced Simon of Cyrene to carry the cross?[19] They must have thought Jesus would die before getting to Calvary. It seems that everyone had given up on Jesus at this point: the crowds, His friends, the Apostles, and even the soldiers. I wonder if Jesus was tempted to give up, too. Why get up the third time and prolong the inevitable? Why not say, "I've endured enough!" Jesus knows He is going to die anyway. What's the difference between dying under the weight of the cross and dying on the cross? The difference is *you!* Jesus' perseverance demonstrates His persevering love for you. Love proves itself with sacrifice.

Jesus, so close to death, fully gives of Himself. He chooses the fullness of the passion because He chooses to completely love man. He falls under the weight of sin three times, but three times He gets up out of love for you. It was sin that tripped Him, but love that lifted Him. Look upon the knees of Christ. They are bloodied, scraped, and worn. The knees of the King of Kings are wounded because they bended for you!

Jesus makes His way to Calvary, passing the mocking crowds, demeaning words of insult hurled His way. People are laughing and staring upon Him as an object of violent entertainment. He was offering His life for them, with their name upon His cross. What interior anguish, to know the gift of self-sacrifice is rejected by so many? Grace that cost so much would be so ignored.

Do we remember we are part of that sneering mob? The words of insult we direct toward others, the interior speeches we preach in judgment, the prejudice we harbor in our hearts, all land on the suffering Christ, making His cross even heavier. Yet no words of rebuke passed from His lips. He carried His cross in silence for all the times we should have been. He held His tongue for all the times ours went out of control. His humble obedience atoned for our reckless words. Do we realize the costly grace poured upon us everyday, granting us the opportunity to speak charitably about others? This gift flows from the cross.

Oh what costly grace, given so recklessly to me.

Love Held Him on the Cross

On the hill of Calvary Jesus is stripped, stretched, and nailed to the wood. His body is raised up on the cross. He is defenseless and exposed, suffering a most humiliating death. The chief priests and teachers below mock Him and among themselves say, "He saved others; he cannot save himself!"[20] The crucifixion seems a paradox.

I think back to the time when Jesus raised up a man named Lazarus. He had been dead for four days by the time Jesus arrived at his tomb. With a loud voice Jesus called,

> "Lazarus, come out!"[21] The dead man came out,
> his hands and feet bound with bandages, and his
> face wrapped with a cloth. Jesus said to them,
> "Unbind him, and let him go." [22]

With three words Jesus had raised a man from the dead. Couldn't He have said another three words to save Himself? Couldn't He have said, "Nails come out!" Which is easier, to raise somebody from the dead or tell nails to move? One can only conclude that it was not nails holding Jesus to the cross, but the power of His love.

"Christ died for our sins in accordance with the scriptures."[23] He atoned for our faults and made satisfaction for our sins to the Father.[24] He chose the nails because He chose to love us. His perfect obedience to God the Father is a substitute for our disobedience, so that we can share in His life.

ৡৢ

The passion of Jesus reveals His passionate love. If you were the only person in the entire world, Jesus still would have freely laid down His life. He still would have given His last breath for you. What amazing love!

If you pass by a mirror today, you will see a face staring back at you. How do you feel about that person? Do you like what you see? Jesus does. In fact, I am sure He would whisper, "You are to die for!" It is true! You are also to rise for.

You were on the mind of Jesus as the crown of thorns was placed upon His head. Your name was upon His lips as He was being crucified, saying, "Father, forgive them; for they know not what they do."[25] You were on His heart when the nails were in His hands. And when Jesus said, "I thirst,"[26] He thirsted for you.

Next time you see a crucifix, remember the words of Jesus on the cross, "It is finished."[27] It was all done for you.

Chapter Four

Becoming The Beloved

Truly, truly, I say to you,
unless one is born of water and the Spirit,
he cannot enter the kingdom of God.
⯎John 3:5⯎

Imagine that you were leaving your loved ones and wouldn't be able to see them again in this life. What would your conversation be like? Hopefully at that point the weather wouldn't be the topic of conversation. Would you choose your words carefully and perhaps communicate what is most important?

The Apostles and Jesus were in that position before He ascended to heaven. Jesus knew that the last conversation was coming. So what did He have to say to the ones He loved, the ones who would carry out His mission? He must have chosen His words carefully. He didn't say, "Go heal people," "Keep on raising the dead," or "Plant a church." Nothing is wrong with these actions, but these are not what Jesus mentioned as the first step in continuing His mission. It was:

> Go therefore and make disciples of all nations, baptizing them in the name of the Father and of the Son and of the Holy Spirit, teaching them to observe all that I have commanded you.[1]

If baptism was such a priority for Jesus, it should be a priority to us. (We will focus on the teaching command of Jesus in a later chapter.)

My brother Keith is a funny guy. I often wondered if he would ever get married because he never took his relationships with girls too seriously. It seemed that he was always more interested in himself than any girl who held an interest in him. Then one day, shortly after he had graduated from university, I received an unexpected email from him describing a girl:

> Her name is Janelle. A mutual friend of ours set us up and *wabang*, it works out. 3 dates in 4 days! And to describe her... I'd have to say she's amazing! She isn't just another pretty face, but a person who I didn't think existed but in my most perfect of dreams. There is so much more to this girl than any words can say; depth, dynamics, and kindness only scratch the surface to what makes Janelle the person she is!
>
> We spent the whole day together yesterday. From 2:30pm to 10:30pm! It was all good! All of it!
>
> Now, I've been on my share of dates, and none have been as wonderful. We shared a lot together and discovered that our views and values are very much the same. She has a very strong faith in God and has Jesus as the center of her life. When I said this girl was amazing, I really wasn't kidding.

> For now I will enjoy this moment that she and
> I have started to share together and hope that it
> lasts...forever.

No joke, this is what he wrote. At first I thought he was delusional and later found out he was just sick ... love sick.

Their relationship blossomed, and months later I found myself standing beside him at the front of the church. He was getting married. Keith looked into the eyes of his bride-to-be and pronounced his marriage vows. She in turn did the same.

Through the sacrament of marriage they entered into a covenant relationship. This is more than a contract or a simple verbal agreement. It is an exchange of persons that forms a family bond. They came into the church, two separate people in love, and left married, no longer their own but belonging to each other. All that my brother is belongs to his wife, and all that she is belongs to my brother. In the words of Jesus, "They are no longer two but one flesh."[2]

The Church teaches that we are the bride of Christ.[3] God doesn't want to be just our buddy; He wants to be our one love. He desires a covenant marriage-like relationship with us.

The First Step Toward Salvation

Just as in marriage there is an exchange of persons, so too is there in a covenant relationship with God. Baptism is the first step in accepting this exchange. We are born into the world without the life of God and the possibility of friendship with Him. This is called original sin.[4] Jesus conquered all sin through His life, death, and resurrection.[5] The benefits of His sacrifice are offered to us through the reception of baptism. Remember that a covenant relationship includes an exchange of persons and a family bond. Baptism imparts the life of Christ's grace into one's soul, erasing original sin, and he becomes an adopted child of God.[6] Christ lives in the newly baptized person, and that person is now part of God's family. This sets us on the path to become "one flesh" with Christ and to grow in a marriage-like relationship with Him.

Check your heart and you'll find in it a longing to be someone of value. People have gone to great lengths in hopes of finding some sort of significance. Credit cards are maxed in an attempt to buy an identity with clothes. We spend hours at the office to achieve a position of distinction. Young women starve themselves; young men take muscle enhancement drugs; while those who are older get plastic surgery; all falsely believing their worth is in their looks. We live vicariously through celebrities and the red carpet dream, believing fame brings significance.

The popular message is "if you have much, you are much," and "if you have little, you are little." If you look great, you are great, and if you look out of style, you are out of style. Many live as though the measure of their significance depends on the measure of their power, money, appeal or fame. The gospel of our time is "the more one has, the more one is." Unfortunately, many accept and give their whole lives to these messages, not knowing they are living for a lie.

We would do well to begin seeing significance through the eyes of God. For Him, value is not a passing fad like bell-bottoms. It doesn't come in a brand name like Calvin Klein. It comes in His name:

At the name of Jesus every knee should bow, in

heaven and on earth and under the earth, and every tongue confess that Jesus Christ is Lord, to the glory of God the Father.[7]

Now that's significance!

Become Part of the Family

There are certain family names that carry a type of eminence, such as Kennedy, Rockefeller and Gates. But those bearing these names will never share their inheritance with you. You will never be their flesh and blood, nor will they adopt you as their child. This probably comes as no surprise. But the eminence of God's name is different than every other name. For one thing, His name will last forever because His Kingdom will not have an end. And the good news is that He shares His name with you and adopts you as His child through baptism. He gives His flesh and blood through the Eucharist, and His eternal glory is your inheritance!

Our value doesn't come from the clothes on our backs, our achievements or our looks. Our value comes from God alone, having been created by and for Him. We begin to embrace this through baptism. No wonder Jesus says, "Go therefore and make disciples of all nations, baptizing them in the name of the Father and of the Son and of the Holy Spirit."[8]

Jesus was someone who knew His significance and from where it came. He was God the Father's only Son. When Jesus was baptized in the River Jordan and had come out of the water, the Father spoke and said, "You are my Son, the Beloved; with you I am well pleased."[9] His identity was affirmed. He was His Father's beloved. Everything that Jesus did flowed out of this relationship. Jesus said, "I and the Father are one,"[10] and "I do nothing on my own, but I speak these things as the Father instructed me."[11] Every word He spoke, each action He carried out, all that He accomplished, resulted because Jesus was in relationship with His Father, knowing He was the Beloved.

How many people would love to hear those same words – that Jesus heard from His heavenly father – from their earthly father? Sadly, for many it will not happen. Broken homes, broken relationships, torn families, uncontrollable circumstances, and death leave many hearts never *knowing* the words "I love you." This causes a wound running deep within the soul, leaving many individuals wondering whether they are even lovable. Maybe you are aware of that pain within yourself. Do you realize that the words spoken to Jesus in the Jordan are also spoken to you? *You* are the beloved of the heavenly Father, and He offers you more than any earthly father could ever give.

In the busyness and bigness of the world, we can easily feel swallowed up and forgotten. There are six and a half billion people here on earth. You are one of them. And out of the six and a half billion, God the Father has His eyes on you. If you find yourself forgetting this, read Psalm 139. It speaks of His personal love: He knows when you sit and stand, the words on your tongue even before you speak them, and the thoughts running through your mind. He sees all of you, knows all about you, and loves every part of you, because you are His child.

You Were Planned by God

God the Father chose you when He planned creation.[12] In all that He has made, from the farthest galaxy to the smallest microscopic cell, He carefully designed to bring you into this world. He knit you together in your mother's womb, and thinks, "Wonderful!" when He thinks of you. He brought you forth on the day you were born and never ceases calling you to rest in His love.[13] If you're going to surrender to any hands, surrender to those which created you, for they know exactly what you need.

God the Father loves us as we are, even though we are not what we should be. His love for us is unconditional. That means there is no condition you could get yourself into that would cause God to find you unlovable. It also means that there is no condition you could work up to that would make you more lovable. His grace comes to us freely, such as in infant baptism, but a free gift often causes problems for us. We are not used to receiving generous gifts. We live in consumer times where nothing is for free, and if it is we ask, "What's the catch?" But God's love is freely given. No amount of good works, prayers, or sacrifices could get God to love us more. That doesn't mean works and prayer are unimportant. They can strengthen or destroy one's relationship with God, but they do not affect His love for us.

Imagine a father holding his newborn in his arms. He stares down upon his baby in awe and wonder, overwhelmed with love, all the while making goo-goo gaga noises as if the child understands. This seems like illogical love, but what do I know, I'm not a father, yet. All that the baby is going to do for the next year is cause sleepless nights, scream at unusually high pitches, and be completely dependent on its parents for everything. This state continues in some families for eighteen years [smiling]. The father doesn't hold the baby in his arms and say, "I love you because I'll never have to mow the grass again." He holds his baby and simply says, "I love you." Period. Likewise, God the Father does not hold us and say, "I'll only love you if you follow my commandments." He simply holds us and says, "I love you," even if we reject His commands.

Baptism brings us into communion with God and His family. We do not stand alone. Since we are children of God in Christ, we also have brothers and sisters in Christ. These include those in the world who have been baptized, those being purified in purgatory, and those in heaven who share more fully in the life of God. If you struggle with loneliness, remember that you are surrounded by saints, a cloud of witnesses who are praying for you to grow in the grace of holiness by remaining faithful to your baptism.[14]

Prime Real Estate

If you could build a dream home anywhere, where would it be? I can think of many beautiful places I would love to have a permanent address. I've climbed to the tops of mountains, in The Rockies where the panoramic view is breathtaking. I've sat on the cliffs of Ireland, with the power of the sea breaking below me. I've fished on secluded northern lakes in the rugged Canadian Shield, where the closest *7-11* is an hour-and-a-half boat ride plus a six-hour drive away. I've snorkeled on Caribbean coral reefs, in crystal clear water surrounded by thousands of colorful fish. And I've hiked the Black Forest of Niagara. The earth is filled with the glory of God! All of these places would be on my top ten locations to build my dream home.

But what if we ask God this question? His options are endless. Consider all the earth, then the entire universe and all the galaxies, all as prime real estate. His possibilities exceed our comprehension. Yet with all these choices before Him, there is only one place He desires to make His home. This place is within you! God has chosen you, over all that He has made, to make His dwelling place. He makes your body not just His dream home, but a temple of the Holy Spirit.[15] And we are not talking about a temporary cottage, good for a few years; He desires to abide in you forever!

The fact that God has chosen you as His eternal temple over all that He has made gives you significance. This truth alone should set you free from all insecurity. You are of infinite worth in His eyes. You are more treasured than anything that has been created in the material world. You are more valued than the sum of everything upon this earth, contained in our galaxy, and each universe combined. You are the summit of the visible creation.[16]

Baptism makes us partakers of His Divine nature, members of Christ and co-heirs with Him.[17] What Christ has, He shares with you! Who Christ is, is offered to you! What an exchange! We give Him rags; He gives us His royalty. We give Him our sin; He gives us His sonship. Baptism is not a legalist, meaningless ritual, but the greatest gift a person could receive. It is the gift of God Himself who draws us to eternal life.

I have another brother named Dave who is also married. Dave is a gentleman. When he proposed to his wife, Kristin, he did it in style. He set up candles all over the basement of our house, prepared a fine meal, and even wrote her a song. Then in a smooth motion of grace he got upon one knee, presented a sparkling diamond ring, and asked Kristin to be his wife. Imagine if Kristin had said no. How that would have pained Dave's heart. What disappointment. He finally finds the woman of his dreams, someone with whom he longs to share the rest of his life, and his love falls on one who would not have it.

The pain of love not received is great pain indeed, and how much more our heavenly Father experiences it. He has found somebody He wants to spend all eternity with. He has found the person of His dreams. His heart has been taken by one with whom He longs to share His very life. And that person is you. But love cannot be forced, only chosen. He has already chosen you; have you chosen Him?

We Are Baptized for Conversion

The grace of baptism is an invitation to love. Just as love cannot be forced, neither can cooperation with the grace of baptism be forced. Just as one cannot say, "You must marry me," God will not say, "You must accept me." God gives us the choice to cooperate and accept His grace, present in this sacrament, or to reject it.

Some misinterpret baptism as a magical formula for salvation. The "now I got done, now I can get in" attitude completely misses the point of baptism. Wouldn't it be silly for a person to get married and then never again place his eyes upon the one he married for the rest of his life? Would that person not be at risk of losing that relationship? Even more ridiculous is for us to receive baptism for the purpose of gaining heaven, but never again in our earthly life to look upon Christ. Would we not also be at risk of losing what we had received in the sacrament if it were not nourished?

Through baptism we are offered new life in Christ, but

that is just the beginning! We need to access this new life through growing in faith. Just as a married couple should continually say "I do" to each other through words and actions, we too, who are baptized, must continually reaffirm our faith by saying "I do" to Jesus through our words and actions.

> The faith required for baptism is not a perfect and mature faith, but a beginning that is called to develop. The catechumen or the godparent is asked: 'What do you ask of God's Church?' The response is: 'Faith!'[18]

What does this faith call us to do? "By faith, man freely commits his entire self to God, making the full submission of his intellect and will to God."[19]

Fr. Cantalamessa is the preacher to the Papal Household. His responsibility over twenty years has been to preach to Pope John Paul II, and more recently to Pope Benedict XVI, on Fridays during Advent and Lent. If two popes have trusted him to preach to them for spiritual nourishment, then what he says can be trusted. He says this, regarding baptism:

> For most of us, baptism is a bound sacrament. That means that while we have received baptism in the church, the church gave it in the hope that at some point in our adult life we would confirm our "I believe" in a personal, free act of faith. Until there is this act of faith in the life of a Christian, baptism remains a bound sacrament.[20]

I don't remember my baptism because I was a baby. My mom and dad had the responsibility of forming my faith, and I have to say they did a fantastic job. But just as you can lead a horse to water but you cannot make him drink, so too was I led through the waters of baptism, by the graciousness of my parents, but I had to make my own personal profession of faith myself. That does not mean my infant baptism was ineffective; however, looking back, I can see that I most often chose not to cooperate with the grace of conversion until I was eighteen years old.

We are baptized for conversion. In the words of Pope John Paul II:

> Conversion means accepting, by a personal decision, the saving sovereignty of Christ and becoming his disciple. The Church calls all people to [this].[21]

Conversion is not a feeling or an emotional high; it is a choice. It requires personally accepting Jesus' death and resurrection. It includes an act of the will, relying on God and His teachings. It also means acknowledging the sinful areas of the heart, asking for forgiveness for these, turning from them, and trusting that God's ways are better than our own. It means becoming another Jesus.

Salvation is always a gift of the Holy Spirit. This truth is emphasized through infant baptism. The baby baptized is completely incapable of believing or doing anything on its own to grow in the life of God. The grace of conversion which leads to eternal life is a free gift that is available to that baby and to all. It makes possible for us a response of faith. We are still completely incapable of believing on our own, but God makes available, always and everywhere, the grace necessary for all to know Him.

The Invitation is His, the Choice is Ours

Are you baptized? If not, why delay? God is longing to make His home within your soul. He is looking for an invitation. Receiving the sacrament of baptism is the first step in responding to God's call in your life. If this is you, contact a Catholic church and ask about the process involved in being baptized. You will have to take classes to gain a deeper knowledge of faith, which you will profess as your own at your baptism.

If you have been baptized, are you cooperating with the sacramental graces, or are the graces bound? God lives within you, but are you allowing Him to have His way? Is Jesus your reigning Lord, or are you reigning over Jesus?

❧

It is hard to understand how He allows us to have our way with the temple He has created, but that is love. It gives one the option to love back. The choice is yours. What will you choose?

Chapter Five

Made For Freedom

*Therefore confess your sins to one another,
and pray for one another, that you may be healed.*
❧ James 5:16 ❧

*My mercy is so great that no mind,
be it of man or of angel,
will be able to fathom it throughout all eternity.*
❧ Diary of St. Faustina ❧

A clean conscience is a happy soul. An example of this is the story of little Robby and his older sister, Sally, summer-vacationing on their Grandpa's chicken farm. Robby had just received a bow and arrow, which his Grandpa had made out of the willow trees in the backyard. Grandpa had bent the willow stick and tied the ends with bailer twine, holding the bow in shape. He gave it to Robby, along with a few straight twigs to serve as his arrows, and said, "Take it down to the barn and practice shooting at the empty milk cans. You might become a mighty hunter one day."

Robby took his new homemade toy down to the barn with excitement. He found an empty milk can and balanced it on a fence beside the barn, then took a few steps back. Picking up his bow and placing the handmade arrow on the string, he took careful aim. Pulling back on the string, Robby let go. The arrow clumsily fell a few feet in front of him, not even reaching the target. A little surprised, but not discouraged, Robby tried again. Again the arrow dropped in front of him, failing to even reach the milk can. The third try was even worse, with the arrow slipping off the string, falling at his feet. Robby, in tearful frustration, grabbed the arrow, put it on the bowstring and pulled back with all his might, aiming up into the sky. Swoosh! The arrow flew with tremendous speed over the milk can and over the barn. Robby watched in disbelief as it continued to sail across the yard. Then, the unthinkable happened. The arrow landed, hitting Grandpa's prized rooster and killing it.

Robby's heart was pounding. He was going to be in so much trouble. He had to hide it. Racing across the yard, he picked up the rooster and ran over to Grandpa's haystack. "Nobody would find it here," he thought. Robby bent over and quickly made a hole in the hay, then threw the rooster in and covered it up.

Getting up, he looked over his shoulder and was startled. His sister Sally was standing right behind him with her arms crossed, smiling.

"What do you want?" yelled Robby.

"Cock-a-doodle-doo," Sally replied sarcastically, and walked away. Robby's heart sank; she knew about the rooster.

During supper Grandpa asked if Sally could help him weed the garden. Sally replied, "Oh Grandpa, Robby said he wanted to do that this evening."

Then leaning over to Robby, she whispered, "Cock-a-doodle-doo." Robby spent that evening working in the garden while Sally ate ice cream on the deck with Grandpa.

The next day Grandpa, Sally, and Robby were relaxing on the deck. Grandpa, turning toward Sally, asked, "Could you mow the grass in the yard this afternoon?"

Sally cheerfully responded, "Oh Grandpa, Robby said earlier how he wanted to mow the grass for you." Then leaning over to Robby, she whispered, "Cock-a-doodle-doo." That afternoon Robby worked under the hot sun while Sally relaxed in the shade.

This continued for a couple of days: Robby doing his chores plus Sally's every time the rooster's crow was mimicked. Finally, Robby couldn't stand it any longer. He worked up enough courage and approached his Grandpa saying, "Grandpa, you know your special rooster?"

"Yes, Robby," answered Grandpa.

"Well, I accidentally killed it with the bow and arrow you gave me. I hid it in the haystack because I was afraid to tell you. I'm sorry."

Grandpa looked at Robby with compassion and said, "I know Robby, I saw the whole thing from the kitchen window. I was waiting to see if you would tell me the truth ... and how long you would do both yours and Sally's chores."

Hanging onto our mistakes only keeps us in a cage of condemnation. Guilt weighs our hearts down, and heaven forbid if anyone finds out our secrets. And when our mistakes are exposed, we rarely take responsibility; instead, we often try desperately to cover them up.

God Has His Eyes on You

Adam and Eve were not very different from us in how they responded to their mistake. God told them, "The tree of the knowledge of good and evil you shall not eat, for in the day that you eat of it you shall die."[1] You likely know what follows in their story. They were tempted and ate the fruit. They made a mistake and sinned. But notice what they did next.

> [When] they heard the sound of the LORD
> God...the man and his wife *hid* themselves from
> the presence of the LORD God among the trees
> of the garden [emphasis added].[2]

Adam and Eve hid from God. They tried to cover up their mistake. How does one hide from God who is all-powerful, all-knowing and everywhere? They were attempting the impossible.

God's response is even more unusual. "But the LORD God called to the man, 'Where are you?'"[3] Why would God, who is all-powerful, all-knowing and everywhere, be asking Adam and Eve their location? Is it because they had successfully hidden from God? I don't think so. When you play hide-and-seek with the all-knowing God, He always wins. God knew exactly what had happened, where they were, and what was going on. The reason He was asking "Where are you?" was not because He didn't know where Adam and Eve were. God was asking the question in order to give Adam and Eve the opportunity to confess their sin. The question, "Where are you?" was asked out of love and for the benefit of Adam and Eve.

The sacrament of reconciliation is God's invitation for us to confess our sin. It is God's call, asking "Where are you?" Sin is an offense to God.[4] It is very difficult to grow in an intimate relationship with others without dealing with offenses you might have caused them. I am sure you can think of somebody whom you love who has hurt you. The deeper the hurt, the more it affects the relationship. Ignoring the offense can destroy the relationship, especially if the hurtful actions continue over a long period of time. Likewise, it is impossible to grow in a personal relationship with Jesus without dealing with what hurts Him. Less serious sin, called venial sin, weakens our relationship with Christ. Serious sin, called mortal sin, completely destroys our friendship with God. The sacrament of reconciliation gives us the opportunity to restore and strengthen our relationship with God by seeking His forgiveness and healing.

Often with our human relationships, the deeper the offense, the less likely it is the relationship will be restored. This is not so with God. There is no injury so grave that God would not forgive, nor wounds so deep that He could not heal. God is more willing to grant us forgiveness and healing than we are to ask for it. St. Paul knew this truth very well. Before his conversion, he approved of the killing of Christians. Later, after becoming Christian himself, he wrote, "but where sin increased, grace abounded all the more."[5] He knew this truth because he had experienced it.

God's Solution for Our Sin

Jesus gave us the sacrament of reconciliation on the evening of Easter, saying to the Apostles, "Receive the Holy Spirit. If you forgive the sins of any, they are forgiven; if you retain the sins of any, they are retained."[6] Sin weakens or destroys the graces we've received at baptism. Jesus has given us reassurance of His forgiveness through this sacrament.

We have a need for forgiveness. St. Paul reminds us that "all have sinned and fall short of the glory of God."[7] If you don't believe it, imagine a big billboard with your face and name on it at a busy intersection near where you live. What if, at the end of each day, all your deeds appeared in video upon the billboard, and all the main thoughts you dwelt upon were the subtitles? Talk about a reality T.V. show! How comfortable would you feel with your life exposed? If you're like me, and something inside of you cringes, could it be that you are ashamed of some of your thoughts and actions? Maybe part of your lifestyle and thought life doesn't match up with what you know is morally right? If you cringe, then there is sin in your heart. Where there is sin, there is shame.

The reality is, "nothing is covered that will not be revealed, or hidden that will not be known."[8] God knows the secrets of our hearts. The billboard is constantly present to Him. Psalm 69 says, "You know my folly, O God; my guilt is not hidden from you."[9] This should not discourage or make us fearful of God, but rather the opposite. It should move us toward Him with confident faith. Think about it; God knows every sin of our heart, from the biggest, darkest offenses, to the hidden, selfish motivations, and still He loves us. What incredible love. I am sure that if you knew me with full knowledge, as God does, you would never have bought my book! You would see the ugliness of my interior and exterior life. The truth is, we do not have the guarantee of acceptance by others. But isn't it wonderful that the only One whose judgment eternally matters is the One who loves us completely?

Sin Never Fulfills Its Promise

Sin never fulfills its promise. Adam and Eve believed that they would be "like God" if they ate of the fruit. The result of their actions caused a fall from friendship with God. This is always true for us. We are never better off choosing sin, although this is the *false* promise we *often* believe. Sin always – without exception – damages or destroys our friendship with God, who is the source of life. It steals the meaning of our lives away, "for the wages of sin is death:"[10] death to hope, joy, peace, love and to the purpose of our lives.

It is reported that more than one out of every ten people in Canada suffer from depression.[11] Feelings of worthlessness, guilt, deep sadness, and thoughts of death, along with diminished interest in daily activities, and sleep disturbances are some of the many struggles this complex illness brings. I wonder how many people would experience a lessening of symptoms if they encountered the forgiveness of Jesus through the sacrament of reconciliation. I do not mean to suggest that all depression is caused by personal sin. I only know my own experience, and it tells me that an honest confession generally results in an increase of joy and peace in my life.

Years of unconfessed sin eventually erode one's peace of the present moment. A person will not find true fulfillment through a sinful lifestyle. Sin can give quick temporary highs, but they fade as quickly as they come. Drugs, alcohol, pre-marital sex, and selfish living can give immediate gratification. But the promise of fulfillment quickly vanishes, leaving the heart feeling used-up and aching. Over time the aching turns into numbness, and the pain of shame seems normal. Eventually one argues, "If it doesn't feel wrong it must be right," or "It doesn't go against my conscience, so what's the big deal?" But what if your conscience has not been formed? You can distort your feelings of "right" and "wrong" through prolonged habits of sin.

We Don't Decide What Sin Is

Have you ever acted against your conscience, then felt very ashamed, only to find yourself committing the same sin again but not feeling nearly as bad? Unfortunately, I have experienced this many times. The reason is not because the moral standard had suddenly changed; it is because my conscience had been wounded. Sin is not gauged by what we *feel* to be bad. It is the Catholic Church, guided by the Holy Spirit, who teaches us what sin is. Our feelings are sometimes deceiving; the Catholic Church is not. For example, if one feels murder is justifiable, that doesn't make it right, because the Church teaches it is wrong. Similarly, if one feels birth control is acceptable, that doesn't make it right, because the Church also teaches it is wrong.

Thank God for His mercy and patience when He looks upon our sense of right and wrong. We need neither a perfectly formed conscience nor perfect sorrow for our sins to participate in reconciliation. This sacrament is not for the perfect! This sacrament is for all those who acknowledge their weakness and are looking for a Savior. It is a perfect Jesus who we meet in this sacrament. May we let Him heal our imperfections.

Perhaps we are participating in the sacrament of reconciliation regularly. We should then check our motivation for going. True sorrow of sin, or contrition, is a gift of God. By His grace we come to recognize the horrifying nature of sin, and the incredible damage it causes. This grace moves us to desire never to sin again, out of love for God and neighbor. Sorrow for sin should be our main inspiration for confession, but sometimes there are motivations, other than contrition, which bring us to this sacrament. Sometimes we go to excuse our conscience, rather than to seek healing with God. We can't stand the feeling of sin, and that becomes the main reason for confession.

We might not even have an intention for conversion. It may be that "clean slate" feeling we are after, without giving consideration to what repentance is. Sometimes no thought is given to the pain inflicted upon the heart of Jesus caused by our sin. Perhaps we pat ourselves on the back for going to confession, but jump from priest to priest so our pattern of sin cannot be recognized. Maybe flowery, religious language – that would make an archangel blush – is our preferred way of confessing sin, but no change of heart occurs. It is possible that in confession we can fall more in love with appearing saintly than desiring to be a saint. Let us beg God for the gift of a truly sorrowful heart. God knows we need it!

Sin Is Never a Private Affair

Sin always leaves us in isolation. The disobedience of Adam and Eve left them hiding in the trees of the garden. Not only was their relationship with God hurt, but so was their relationship with each other. You cannot have a harmonious relationship with another person if you are fearfully hiding in the bushes. Like Adam and Eve, our sin never weakens only our relationship with God; it also damages our relationship with those around us – the Church.

If you punch somebody in the nose, it is not enough to simply ask God's forgiveness in the privacy of your own home; you should seek forgiveness and healing with the one whom you have hurt. Likewise, sin offends God, but it also wounds the Church to which we belong. Sin is never a private affair, so the forgiveness of it shouldn't be either. Through the sacrament of reconciliation we receive forgiveness from God and also from the Church. You cannot receive this type of healing in the privacy of your own home. "Reconciliation with the Church is inseparable from reconciliation with God."[12]

Some struggle with the thought of going to reconciliation with a priest. Let's change the perception slightly and imagine going to confession with Jesus, not your parish priest, but Christ Himself. The person who died for yours sins will be your confessor. Might your confession change? Might you be more honest as, after all, you do have the Second Person of the Trinity before you? He knows all of your sins already. Why hold anything back?

Most would agree that this would motivate a more honest and contrite confession. The truth is, we encounter Jesus in the sacrament of reconciliation. He is present in the priest through the ministry of the priesthood. Remember that Jesus gave His Apostles the power to forgive sins. "If you forgive the sins of any, they are forgiven; if you retain the sins of any, they are retained."[13] When the priest pronounces the words of absolution, it is as though Jesus Himself is speaking the words, "I absolve you from your sins."[14] What a gift. The priest truly represents Jesus in this sacrament and acts in the person of Christ.[15] The One who loves you completely offers you complete forgiveness in this sacrament.

Forgiveness Leads to Order

Love gives meaning to our lives; without it we are senseless. I remember a young man who attended a large youth retreat I was leading. At the end of the weekend, he came forward and shared how his life had been full of chaos, but after participating in the sacrament of reconciliation and Eucharistic adoration he had found order. That is what God's grace can bring to our lives. Sin leads to chaos; forgiveness leads to order.

Have you ever had an honest reconciliation where you said everything? Are there things hidden in your past that you have never confessed? Why keep it hidden in the haystack and allow your memories to whisper, "Cock-a-doodle-doo!" When we hold onto our sin, we only accuse ourselves and miss the freedom of Jesus' forgiveness.

Our hearts are thirsting for God's love, and we experience His love in this sacrament. No more profoundly do we hear the words "I love you" than when we hear the words "I forgive you." Love proves itself in sacrifice, and there is always a cost in forgiving another. When we are forgiven in this sacrament, the reality of God's sacrificial love is experienced through grace. And grace is costly because it flows from the cross of Jesus. It is one thing to read about it in Scripture or in a book about God's forgiveness, but it is a completely other experience when we ask for the forgiveness of God in an honest confession. The words echoed in the confessional, "I absolve you from your sins," answer our heart's cry, "I need to be loved." Have you allowed yourself to be loved by God in this sacrament with an honest confession?

God is not angry with you. His heart breaks with the knowledge of your sin, just as a father's heart would break if his child ran away. He waits in constant anticipation to release acceptance into your life, but He needs your honesty in this sacrament. "If we confess our sins, he is faithful and just, and will forgive our sins and cleanse us from all unrighteousness."[16]

I speak at many conferences and retreats during the year. On one occasion, I asked my sister Kristy to share her personal faith journey. Below is a small portion of her message which highlights our heavenly Father's forgiveness.

> I [Kristy] was living for partying and staying out all night. My relationship with my parents began to decline dramatically, and I didn't seem to care who I hurt. My parents would try to reach out to me, but I would always push them away. To support my drinking and smoking habits, I stole money from them. My parents worked hard everyday to feed and support our family of seven kids, and yet I took from them. They always gave of themselves, yet somehow I didn't realize their love. All my sin blinded me. I was totally lost, but I didn't realize it. I wanted to do what I wanted and when I wanted.
>
> When I was thirteen years old, I ran away from home. I remember sneaking out in the middle of the night and being picked up by my boyfriend. I wasn't really sure where I was going or what I was going to do, but I knew that I wanted to leave, so I did. We drove to his house which was in another town. A few hours later the cops found us, and my aunt picked me up. On the way home we met up with my father. I'll never forget the look on his face when he saw that I was okay. Instead of yelling at me and scolding

me, all he did was put his hand on my shoulder, and he said to me, "It's good to see you." My parents loved me so much. I am truly thankful for the forgiveness and mercy that Christ has had toward me.

ༀༀ

Listen carefully to your heart. God the Father is calling, "Where are you?" Will you allow yourself to be found in the sacrament of forgiveness? He will not scold you nor will He yell. He's given everything in His Son so that you would be safe. He longs to place His hand of acceptance on your shoulder and whisper words of forgiveness: "It's good to see you." He is waiting.

Chapter Six

It Can't Get Better!

There is nothing so great as the Eucharist.
If God had something more precious,
He would have given it to us.
❧Saint Jean Vianney❧

Take, eat; this is my body.
❧ Matthew 26:26 ❧

During my university days, I sometimes attended a protestant young adults' worship evening on Tuesday nights. I always enjoyed the worship and felt encouraged by the preaching given by their dynamic young adults' pastor. After one of these meetings, I was standing at the back of the gym when a young man approached me. I had met him before through a mutual friend.

"You're Ken, right?" he said as he reintroduced himself.

I straightened my shoulders and answered, "Yes, I am."

"You mean, you're Catholic Ken?" Apparently the word was getting around that I was Catholic. I never hid the fact of which church I attended.

"Yes," I responded smiling. "I am Ken, and I am Catholic."

He paused, squinted his eyes, and asked, "So, are you one of those transubstantiation guys?"

I began to get the feeling there was an agenda behind his questions. "Yes, I am," I responded.

"You mean to tell me that you believe you receive the body and blood of Jesus when you go to church?"

Without any hesitation I replied, "Yes, I do."

In curious unbelief, he asked, "Tell me this, if *that* is Jesus, and people in your church are touching Him *every* Sunday, how come their lives aren't being changed?"

The question silenced me. I don't remember what I said to him in response, but I remember choosing to believe two thousand years of firm teaching rather than being swayed by my inability to defend what I knew to be true. Still, what a great question! If that is Jesus, and we are touching the living Savior, His body, blood, soul and divinity, how come our lives aren't being changed?

I took this to prayer and remembered the Gospel account of a woman who had been hemorrhaging for twelve years. She had spent all her money on doctors, but nobody could cure her. As Jesus walked through the crowds, the woman who had been bleeding said to herself, "If I only touch his garment, I shall be made well."[1]

> She came up behind him and touched the fringe of his clothes, and immediately her haemorrhage stopped. Then Jesus asked, 'Who touched me?' When all denied it, Peter said, 'Master, the crowds surround you and press in on you.'[2]

Jesus' question, "Who touched me?" seems silly, considering the circumstance. The crowds were almost crushing him.[3] There were many people touching Jesus. Even Peter pointed this out, likely because he was getting crushed, too. But Jesus knew something Peter did not. Within the crowd there was one person who had touched Him *with faith!*

> When the woman saw that she could not remain hidden, she came trembling; and falling down before him, she declared in the presence of all the people why she had touched him, and how she had been immediately healed. He said to her, "Daughter, your faith has made you well; go in peace."[4]

Why was the woman healed? It wasn't because she had touched Jesus; it was because she had faith in the One she had touched!

Desperation Births Transformation

Why aren't our lives being changed when we receive Jesus in the Eucharist? Could it be because we don't have desperate faith in Jesus like the woman who was healed? A typical practicing Catholic goes to mass on Sunday and receives the Eucharist. Are we one of those in the crowd who simply bumps into Jesus at mass as He passes by, or do we have faith in Him to change our lives? We are not just touching the "tassel of his cloak," we are touching Jesus Himself, the One who died and rose for our salvation. We touch *Jesus.* How much more faith should we have than the woman who touched the tassel?

Desperation births transformation. The lady who was healed was desperate. "She had spent all she had on physicians, no one could cure her."[5] Now she had nothing but her faith:

no more money, no more security. It was in this empty state that she approached Jesus.

Only when we abandon our securities and become hungry for Jesus, will He move in us with transforming power. Our faith must rest in Him alone. "Blessed are those who hunger and thirst for righteousness, for they shall be satisfied."[6] Jesus is righteousness Himself. Are we hungry for Him when we attend mass?

When participating in the mass, we must have desperation for Jesus as though our life depends upon Him. Approach Him as if your very breath would cease without Him. We must come to Him this way because it is true. We are incapable of living without His grace. Jesus said:

> He who abides in me, and I in him, he it is that bears much fruit, for apart from me you can do *nothing* [emphasis added].[7]

Nothing means *nothing*. We could not even move our little finger without the grace of God. We forget our dependence on Him, in a world that insists on independence. We play God, trying to take control of the future and direction of our lives. We mistakenly believe that we can make a difference in the world. This is not so. It is God's grace that allows us to accomplish even the smallest good, whether we acknowledge this or not. All that is good and beautiful originates from God. All is grace!

We must remain in His love because without Him we are a "noisy gong or a clanging cymbal."[8] So how do we abide in His love? Jesus answers this when speaking about the Eucharist. "He who eats my flesh and drinks my blood *abides* in me and I in him [emphasis added]."[9] If we wish to have an impact on others and "bear much fruit," we should come to our Eucharistic Jesus and abandon our lives to Him.

Acknowledge your nothingness before Jesus, and He will give you everything by offering Himself in this sacrament. To find importance, come to the important One. To grow in significance, come receive the significant One. To find eternal happiness, receive the eternal One. It is He whom you receive in the Eucharist. Jesus allows you to consume Him so that He is allowed to consume you.

The Greatest Event in History, Made Present

Events shape culture. The rise and fall of monarchies, wars, the signing of peace treaties, the assassination of leaders, scientific discoveries, and natural disasters are only some events that have influenced our world in the recent past. If you had to pick the most important event in history, what would it be? Would it be an invention or a person? The rise of a philosophy or the demise of one? The choices are endless, but for the Christian the answer should be clear. The most important and greatest event in history is the Paschal mystery.[10]

You may be wondering what the Paschal mystery is. It's the term the Church uses to describe Jesus Christ's saving mission. It has two aspects: the death and the resurrection of Jesus. "By his death Christ liberates us from sin; by his Resurrection, he opens for us the way to a new life."[11] Not only does this event shape our time now, but it affects all eternity. The death and resurrection of Jesus affects every single man, woman, and child on the face of the earth now, and everyone who has ever lived. No other event compares to this.

If you had an opportunity to be present at Calvary two thousand years ago, how would you feel? What would be running through your mind, as you see your Savior Jesus hanging on the cross? Would you not respond with tremendous reverence, knowing you're at the place of your salvation? You might be moved with praise and thanksgiving, or brought to repentance, seeing the horrifying nature of sin. Whatever your response, I am sure Jesus would have your attention and your heart. I am also positive that we could agree this would be a tremendous privilege – to be present at the greatest event in history – and given the opportunity, you would not miss it.

Did you know that Jesus made His sacrifice of Calvary present for you today? It likely happened down the street, not far from where you are reading this book. Did you miss it? This opportunity is called mass. The Eucharist "makes present and actual the sacrifice which Christ offered to the Father on the cross."[12] When we attend mass, Calvary is made present to us! This is what happens through the liturgy. Mass makes present the greatest event in history.

No wonder the Church refers to the Eucharist as the "source and summit of all Christian life."[13] "The Eucharist is the very sacrifice of the Body and Blood of the Lord Jesus."[14] In the words of St. Thomas Aquinas, "The celebration of the Holy Mass is as valuable as the death of Jesus on the Cross."[15] The mass deserves our reverence because Jesus deserves our reverence. It is He who is truly present at mass in the Eucharist.

The Commands of God Meet Our Needs

Sometimes, when another commands us to do something, we think, "This person is controlling and domineering." "Who are they to tell me what to do?" "What are they getting out of this?" Often our reaction is to get angry and defensive. We shut them out, becoming closed to their ideas. We focus on the cost to ourselves and judge their motivation.

Often we project this attitude on God when He commands us to do something. We forget that God is all-powerful and lacking nothing. We misunderstand that when God makes a command it is always for the benefit of those to whom He speaks. Realize if God commands you to do something, it is not because He is lacking something; it is because *you* lack something, and His request will meet your need. This knowledge should give you tremendous freedom to obey! The commands of God meet our needs; therefore, we should not fight obedience to Him.

In the Gospels, Jesus commanded His Apostles and those listening to do something that was for their benefit, but many refused. In John 6, Jesus said, "Truly, truly, I say to you, unless you eat the flesh of the Son of man and drink his blood, you have no life in you."[16] And to make sure they understood that it was His literal flesh and blood He was speaking of, again Jesus said, "For my flesh is food indeed, and my blood is drink indeed."[17] As a result, many of His disciples left him.[18]

A few hours before His death, Jesus commands His Apostles to do something. He took some bread, blessed it, and gave it to His Apostles saying:

> "Take, eat; this is my body." And he took a cup, and when he had given thanks he gave it to them, saying, "Drink of it, all of you; for this is my blood of the covenant."[19]

Jesus said to take and eat His body and drink His blood. This, He commands of you, too. We fulfill this command at mass when we receive the Eucharist, which is to the benefit of our salvation.

Today, people often approach Sunday mass as something they have to check off their list to be a good Catholic. The prevailing attitude is just sit back and it will be over in an hour. If we truly knew the graces that we miss with this attitude, we would die from regret.

Jesus is offering His very self to us in this sacrament. It can't get better than this. What can improve is our response. Through the Eucharist, Jesus surrenders all that He is into our hands in hopes that we would surrender all that we are back into His.

Renewing Our Covenant Relationship with God

Recall in Chapter Four on baptism that God wants a covenant relationship with us. This results in a family bond. I am the oldest of seven children. Part of the family bond the seven of us share comes through the Yasinski family name we were born into. Through baptism, we are born into the family of God and receive His family name, being baptized "In the name of the Father, Son, and Holy Spirit."

But there is more than a family name that I share with my brothers and sisters. We share flesh and blood, because we come from the same parents. Likewise, God is not content with just giving us His name; He also wants to give us His flesh and blood to deepen our family bond with Him. When we receive the Eucharist at mass, we are renewing this covenant relationship.

My Grandparents have been married for sixty years. Their anniversary celebration was planned for this past summer, where they renewed the marriage vows they first made more than half a century ago. Much has changed since then, but not their commitment to each other. Their "I do" then is still alive now.

When you were baptized as an infant, your parents and Godparents said, "I do," on your behalf. This brought you into a covenant, marriage-like relationship with God. When you receive the Eucharist at mass, you are renewing this relationship. It is like renewing marriage vows. Much might have changed since you were baptized, but God's commitment to you hasn't.

Next time you go to mass and receive the Eucharist, don't go up because you're the next one in line. Take the opportunity to give yourself entirely back to Jesus to renew your covenant with Him.

The blessings of receiving the Eucharist are many. Through it we receive the flesh and blood of Jesus, renewing our relationship with God and His Church. It protects and renews the graces we received at baptism and confirmation, and it makes us grow in the gift of love, since we receive love Himself. Finally, venial sins are wiped away, and we receive strength to persevere over serious sin.

The Best of the Best

The best that God the Father could give is offered in Jesus through the Eucharist. In this sacrament, God will give us all the graces we need, for in it is contained "the whole spiritual good of the Church, namely Christ himself."[20] St. Augustine, when speaking about this sacrament, said:

> Although God is all-powerful, He us unable to give more; though supremely wise, He knows not how to give more; though vastly rich, He has not more to give.[21]

It is a tragedy not to receive the best gift of God the Father. Therefore, the Church in her wisdom requires that to be a faithful Catholic one must attend mass every Sunday.

The Sunday obligation is not meant to restrict you, but rather, give you freedom. Freedom is not the ability to do whatever you want, when you want it. This leads to bondage. Adam and Eve chose the fruit over God's desire for them, and they lost friendship with God. Freedom is the grace to be obedient to God in all things. Since living a Jesus-centered life gives meaning to our lives, then living a Eucharistic-centered life will do the same. To be truly Jesus-centered is to be Eucharistic-centered. Going to mass on Sunday will bring freedom and meaning to your life. It is of infinite value to your soul. It would be senseless not to want to receive this gift.

To love another is to desire the highest good for them. When you receive Jesus at mass, you are loving yourself, because He is the greatest good for your soul. You also are loving Jesus, because you are obeying His command to "take and eat." And finally, you are loving the Church, since by receiving the Eucharist you are reinforcing the unity of the Church as the Mystical Body of Christ and gaining grace for the world.[22]

St. Francis of Assisi said:

> Man should tremble, the world should vibrate, all Heaven should be deeply moved when the Son of God appears on the altar in the hands of the priest.[23]

The Infinite One becomes present for you at mass. Are you present for Him? Are you attending mass every Sunday with your heart? This is your duty and great privilege. At mass is where you will find the purpose of your soul. Attend holy mass with all your heart, and you will discover the heart of God.

Chapter Seven

A Life-Giving Choice

As the Lord has forgiven you, so you also must forgive.
Colossians 3:13

To forgive is to set a prisoner free
and discover the prisoner was you.
Lewis B. Smedes

A gifted young man full of ambition had his heart set on attending a graduate school in Tokyo. It was his dream to attend this prestigious university in order to eventually climb the ladder of success. However, all his dreams were crushed when his application was denied. His once hopeful future seemed bleak. Unable to deal with the rejection, he became obsessed with this minor set-back. In his mind there was one person responsible for his lost opportunity: a professor working at the university. He directed all his anger and bitterness towards this prof. He called the professor an average of ten times a day, between the hours of 8:00 p.m. and 2:00 a.m. ... for fourteen years! After over a decade of obsessive resentment, and a total of fifty thousand phone calls, the once-young man was arrested by police and put in jail.

It was resentment, and not a professor, that stole this young man's future. If only he would have chosen at the beginning to let go of the past, he could have found freedom in the present, opening the way for a promising future. Imagine the hours and energy wasted. Wouldn't it have been easier to have said the words "I forgive you?"

Forgiveness Is a Decision

To forgive is one of the most important decisions we will ever have to make. Through this choice we communicate to God the way we wish to be treated by Him. We will either live according to the law of judgment or the law of grace. The law of judgment says, "If you hurt me, I am going to hurt you." It is by this system that many people in the world operate. It seems fair. The problem is you end up with two hurt people who want judgment for the other but grace and healing for themselves. We cannot live by two laws. It's one or the other. Jesus said:

> Judge not, and you will not be judged; condemn not, and you will not be condemned; forgive, and you will be forgiven.[1]

Do we give grace, or do we give judgment? What we give is what we will receive.

So many people are living bitter-tasting lives, and they don't have to. God doesn't create bitter people. People choose bitterness. It is a choice to hang onto the past and be resentful. One can choose to forgive or hang onto resentment. Living by the law of grace is the path by which we will find true peace in life. It says, "If you hurt me, I will love you as God loves," meaning, "I forgive you." When we live according to this principle, we allow ourselves to receive freedom from our own shame and guilt. Jesus reminds us, "For if you forgive men their trespasses, your heavenly Father also will forgive you."[2] Forgiveness is the antidote for all sin committed by us and against us.

To experience intimacy with God requires that we forgive others. Forgiveness is not an option.

> In refusing to forgive our brothers and sisters, our hearts are closed and their hardness makes us [resistant] to the Father's merciful love.[3]

Don't let the sin of others keep you from the mercy of the Father. Jesus warns us of this: "If you do not forgive men their trespasses, neither will your Father forgive your trespasses."[4] God is always willing to forgive us, but we close ourselves to His forgiveness if we do not extend forgiveness to those who have sinned against us.

Normally we have no control over whether others sin against us or not, but we do have control over how we respond to their offenses. When we are sinned against, we carry a cost for others' sins. Ultimately, their actions cost us our peace. Since they took peace from us, this is what they owe us. In one sense, a debt owing against them is incurred at our expense. Forgiveness surrenders to Jesus the right to collect on that debt of pain. We do have the ability to get even with a person, but forgiveness means laying down the right of revenge. This does not mean what they did was right. It means we are free from the burden to collect on that debt.

Forgiveness is choosing right by letting go of their wrong. It is a decision of the will to no longer keep score of the past. It gives up the mission to get even or "one up" the offender. When you forgive, you cancel the debt of their sin owed to you, by giving it to Jesus. You let God be the judge. Forgiveness is the best decision you can make.

Forgiveness Leads to Healing

We all have had our bumps and bruises, but don't some of them feel like devastating blows? Painful events of the past still can have power to haunt our present, and the wounds of yesterday seem not to heal with time.

Hurtful experiences in life are inevitable, but to be held captive by their pain is not. We must learn how to react with the heart of God. Our response to another's offense means the difference between staying in hurt or finding healing. When we insist that we are owed, we remain in bondage, and the cost to us actually increases! Not only do we become resistant to God's healing, which alone can restore peace in our lives, but we also allow for more resentment to build upon the initial foundation of hurt. Bitterness breeds bitterness.

"He who sows sparingly will also reap sparingly, and he who sows bountifully will also reap bountifully."[5] The longer we hold to the debt of pain others have caused – generously sowing resentment – the more resentment grows. However, when we choose forgiveness, we accept that Christ's sacrifice has paid in full the wages of sin. This includes the burden of sin we are holding against those who have hurt us. Part of forgiving is acknowledging God Himself has atoned for others' crimes. We must release our claim on the debt of pain and give it Christ. Only when we forgive others the hurt they have caused us can the grace of God begin to heal the wounds of past events.

We must realize that harboring resentment towards others does very little to them and actually hurts us! The book of Hebrews warns:

> See to it that no one fail to obtain the grace of God; that no "root of bitterness" spring up and cause trouble, and by it the many become defiled.[6]

Bitterness causes us to miss out on God's grace. If we want God's purpose for our lives, then we must learn to forgive. We must see, too, that with each judgment towards another we place one more thorn in the crown of Christ. By holding others in judgment, we crucify Christ anew with our hearts. In realizing this, we learn that when we love those who hurt us, we also love Christ. These revelations to our heart make forgiveness much easier.

Forgiveness is the high point of Christian prayer.[7] It shares the love of God with others. It leads us to sow grace and to build a foundation of charity in our lives. To choose to love someone a little bit leads us to love them more. As a person sows, they will also reap.[8] Then sow the gift of love, and love will increase in your life.

Some object to forgiveness, saying, "But they don't deserve it." That may feel true, but love is much more than a feeling; it is a choice. To choose to love when it hurts is to love with Divine love. It hurt Jesus to love us; He was nailed to the cross. This is part of merciful love. If you don't feel they deserve it, you still must choose to give it.

You Will Never Have to Forgive More Than What God Has Forgiven You

There are some who have had tremendous pain inflicted upon them by others, and the prospect of forgiveness seems impossible. If you find yourself in this situation, I encourage you to look at the crucifix. The Roman soldiers weren't the only ones who nailed Jesus to the cross that day. We were the authors of Christ's passion.[9] If Jesus forgives us for playing a part in His crucifixion, then we must forgive those who crucify us. The injustice committed against us who are sinful could never compare to the injustice experienced by the sinless Son of God, yet God forgives us; so then, we must forgive others.

St. Paul reminds us to "be kind to one another, tenderhearted, forgiving one another, as God in Christ forgave you."[10] When we give up the right of revenge, God's grace is allowed to heal the pain others have caused us. When the sins of others wound us, remember "where sin increase[s], grace abound[s] all the more."[11]

We have all had people in our lives who have caused us pain. Don't be surprised that the people you love the most are the ones who have hurt you the most. Family and close friends are the people we spend the most time with and therefore have more opportunity to cause pain.

Signs of Unforgiveness

To forgive another, one has to be able to recognize unforgiveness. Check your heart and see if you are harboring unforgiveness through: holding on to past events that were hurtful; seeking revenge for past wrongs; lying awake at night, upset over the past; having conversations in your head of "telling off" someone; becoming physically ill or distressed when you think of past hurts. These are all signs that you have not extended forgiveness. On the other hand, if you can sincerely pray for the needs of those who have hurt you and be happy for them in their success, these are signs that you truly have forgiven.

If you struggle with unforgiveness toward some people in your life, then acknowledging this is the first step to forgiveness. Sometimes we are reluctant to forgive because of misconceptions about what forgiveness is. It does not mean the offender is excused or pardoned.

On May 13, 1981, Pope John Paul II was shot and critically wounded by Mehmet Ali Ağca, a Turkish gunman. Two years later the pope visited his would-be assassin in an Italian jail and forgave him. The pope did not excuse him. The gunman remained in jail for nearly twenty years serving his sentence.

When you forgive somebody, they still remain accountable for their actions. Forgiveness does not deny justice. Forgiveness does not mean: you have to trust the offender again, that you have to forget the past, or that what they did was okay.

Forgiveness does not leave you with nothing on which to hang; rather, when we forgive, we cling to the grace of God. Hanging onto Jesus is liberating compared to clutching our resentments.

I love climbing mountains. The ascent to the summit is always my goal. Standing on the top of a mountain feels like standing on the top of the world. It is an awesome experience to be surrounded by the majesty and beauty of God's creation, knowing He is infinitely more majestic and beautiful than what is before you. I have climbed many mountains, and while I don't claim to be an expert, I have learned an important thing about the obstacles. The weather can wear you, the climb can drain you, but if you have a pebble in your shoe, you're not going far. At first it feels like a minor annoyance, but over thousands of steps that little pebble creates a major problem. Your foot becomes raw, and it will be the pebble, not the mountain, that defeats you. Little offenses committed against us are the pebbles in our spiritual walk and require our attention.

Forgive the Little Bumps and the Big Ones

A little bitterness over a long period of time can be your defeat. Take, for example, a sarcastic remark by a family member, made in fun but which hurt you. You may not even notice at first how it is affecting your relationship. Loss of patience with them gets chalked up to a bad day. You lose your temper, say a few harsh words, and then rationalize it, saying, "They had it coming." The original unforgiveness is ignored, and the wound festers. Next are more hurtful words, compounded on previous grudges. Your relationship with the person begins to deteriorate. Now there is more to forgive. It seems that it is easier to ignore the person than to communicate with them. The silence actually causes more distance and hurt. You have a major confrontation over something small. You begin judging the other person, saying, "They are always insensitive." You explain your side of the story to others, and they begin picking sides. You avoid each other at family functions; maybe one of you stops going altogether. The relationship is almost destroyed, and others around you are also affected.

Is this an over-exaggeration? I don't think so. Are there relationships in your family that are strained? Is not much of that tension caused by people acting out of bitterness and resentment? Would not forgiveness be the better option? Some are tempted to conveniently brush aside minor slights. They trivialize their hurt by saying, "It was nothing." If it hurt you, it is something. Since it is a little offense, then praise God; it won't be a costly forgiveness. The sooner our resentments are caught, the easier it is to forgive, and the less likely we are to react in a sinful way toward others. Forgive the pebble so it doesn't become the mountain.

Forgiveness is the way of love. And love is the greatest gift. If you ever pray for a greater increase of love, God may answer the prayer by allowing more opportunities to forgive! From the person who cuts you off on the road, or the waiter who got your order wrong, to the one who butts in front of you at *McDonald's*, or the family member who doesn't give phone messages: see all these situations as invitations from God to grow in love by learning to forgive.

There Is an Imperfect Person Wearing Your Shoes

We are surrounded by imperfect people, but remember, there is one who walks in your shoes everyday. Let this keep you compassionate. You are in need of mercy just as much as the people who offend you. Do not demand to receive from God what you will not give to others. You've asked God to treat you this way every time you prayed the Our Father. Recall the line that says, "And forgive us our debts, as we also have forgiven our debtors."[12] Through this prayer, we tell God the Father that the same way we forgive others is how we wish to be forgiven. This is meant to be a comforting prayer, because we are called to be a people of love. If this prayer scares you, then maybe there are people you haven't forgiven.

Take the lead in working at your relationships. Don't wait until others ask for forgiveness before you extend it. Their apology may never happen. Instead, extend forgiveness as soon as the hurt is caused. This is more for your own sake than theirs.

Forgiving another is not cornering them and telling them that you have forgiven their offense. This would likely cause a lot more harm than good. *Don't do it!*

> But when you pray, go into your room and shut the door and pray to your Father who is in secret; and your Father who sees in secret will reward you.[13]

Your prayer of forgiveness is a private prayer. Close your eyes and picture the person standing before you. Speak to them out loud telling them exactly what they did and how they sinned against you. Then say, "I forgive you for _____, and will no longer hold the past against you." You can also write out a prayer letter, detailing the offense and how you give up the right to revenge. In it, sincerely bless the person. Tear up the letter when it's done as a sign of forgiveness.

Some may exclaim, "It is impossible to forgive," or "You don't know what I've been through!" "With men this is impossible, but with God all things are possible."[14] When forgiveness is impossible for us, it is always possible with God. Ask for the grace to forgive. If you can't, then pray for the willingness to forgive. If that is too much, ask for the willingness to want to forgive.

Jesus' commandment, to love one another as He has loved (John 15:12), does seem impossible, but consider this: would it be loving for God to command you to do something He would not help you with? Of course not! When God commands the impossible, it is because He wants to give us His Spirit. True forgiveness that rises from the heart can be accomplished only through the Holy Spirit. By His grace we can accomplish what He asks of us.

It is God's will for you to forgive those who have hurt you. You don't have to discern it! Therefore, be confident He will give what is necessary. Remember who lives within you. The same Jesus who said on the cross, "Father forgive them for they know not what they do,"[15] lives within you. It is also the same Jesus whom you receive in the Eucharist. He is willing to help you. Are you willing to receive His help?

Forgiveness Is Life-Giving

In 1902, a twelve-year-old girl named Maria gave the world an example of love and forgiveness. On July 5, she was sitting on the landing of her home watching over her baby sister. The rest of her family was a short distance away in the field, threshing. A young man named Alessandro, who worked with the family, came in from the field and went into the house. He had been impurely fascinated with Maria and had approached her several times before. He called out to Maria to come into the house. Mistrusting his intentions, she asked why. Alessandro only repeated his demand. Again Maria refused to go without a reason. At this, Alessandro came out and dragged her off the landing into the house. He sexually assaulted Maria as she yelled out, "No! No! Do not touch me!

It is a sin; you will go to hell!" With the hum of the threshing machine in the field drowning out her cries, Alessandro picked up a knife and began to stab her repeatedly. Maria still refused to give in.

Maria was found by her family and rushed to the hospital. Doctors tried desperately to help her, but were unsuccessful. A priest was called to give her Holy Communion. Before giving the host to Maria, he asked if she had forgiven the young man. She responded:

> Yes, I too, for the love of Jesus, forgive him ... and I want him to be with me in Paradise.... May God forgive him because I already have forgiven him. [16]

Maria died shortly after three o'clock. She preferred death over sin.

Alessandro was sentenced to jail where he remained unrepentant for several years. One night he had a dream in which Maria appeared and offered to him fourteen lilies: one for every stab wound. Upon awaking, Alessandro was a changed man. After serving twenty-seven years, he was released and went straight to Maria's mother and begged her forgiveness. Maria's mother responded:

> Alessandro, Marietta forgave you, Christ has forgiven you, and why should I not also forgive? I forgive you, of course, my son! Why have I not seen you sooner? Your evil days are past, and to me, you are a long-suffering son. [17]

The next day they went to mass and received Holy Communion side by side. Alessandro later became a Capuchin lay brother.

On June 24, 1950, Pope Pius XII canonized Maria Gorettii a Saint of the Catholic Church. She is a patron saint of young people, purity, and victims of rape. Standing in the crowd at the canonization were Alessandro and Maria's mother. It was the first time in history a mother was at the canonization of her child.

Maria's forgiveness was life-giving for herself and others. So can be yours. You can accomplish all things through Christ who strengthens you[18] ... even forgiveness.

Chapter Eight

Living With An
Eternal Perspective

*Indeed I count everything as loss
because of the surpassing worth of
knowing Christ Jesus my Lord.*
Philippians 3:8

On the evening of May 25, 1996, at around 8:15 p.m., something happened that changed my life. I was on the small Caribbean Island of St. Lucia with twenty-nine other young adults as part of a mission trip organized by Catholic Christian Outreach (CCO).[1] We were there at the invitation of Archbishop Kelvin Flexi to work with young people.

On this particular evening, the ladies on our team were facilitating a women's retreat at a large house not far from our base parish. I had been requested to join them briefly to participate in a short skit that involved painting my face all white. After the skit, I was washing the paint off when my team leader approached me. She asked that I walk back to the Church where I would be picked up and driven back to our team's accommodations.

I finished washing up and went to leave the house. I had my hand on the door knob when I felt a tap on my shoulder. It was my team leader. She asked, "Where are you going?"

"Back to the church," I responded.

"But we have a rule that nobody walks alone."

"But you said I have to go back to the church to catch my ride," I said, a little confused.

She seemed a bit confused, too, and then asked if she could pray over me for protection. I thought that was rather unnecessary, since it was an eight to ten minute walk back to the Church, but I didn't object. She extended her hand over me, and asked God to send special angels to guard me as I walked back. In my mind I was thinking, "It's a ten-minute walk. What could happen?"

She finished her prayer, and I walked out into the night. I immediately started talking out loud to my guardian angel. It was more a causal conversation than prayer, and if somebody would have seen me, they would have thought, "There's a crazy white guy talking to himself!"

I began to walk down the road, my way lit by the moon. Through the darkness I noticed a spot ahead where there were shadows moving. As drew closer, I could see it was a bunch of wild dogs. I have a strong dislike for dogs. I would say "hate," but that wouldn't be Christ-like. I am scared of them, especially ones I do not know. My first thought was to go around them, but there was thick bush along the side of the road. I determined my two options were 1) turn around and admit to a house full of ladies I'm chicken of dogs, or 2) walk toward the dogs and hope they would move, leaving me alone. There was no way I was going to admit to the ladies my fear of canines, so of course I walked forward.

As I drew closer, the dogs began to bark at me. The closer I got to them the more aggressive they became. I soon found myself stopped right in front of them, unable to go any further because they would not let me pass. The dogs began to circle around me like wolves would circle prey. I stood there in a panic, not knowing what to do. They would approach me, snap, and then pull back. There was one dog much larger than the rest. I kept my eyes on him. As he circled in front of me, he leaned back like he was going to attack. At that moment something very unexpected happened. The word "Jesus" popped out of my mouth. I didn't even mean to say it. As soon as I said His name, all the dogs fled. They went from an aggressive pack to retreating mutts in a second. I couldn't believe what had happened.

My mind jumped back to my team leader's prayer of protection and how I uncharacteristically had been talking to my angel. I knew God had just protected me, and I began to thank and praise Him out loud.

I continued down the road and now could see the church in the distance. I also noticed another point on my path that made me very uneasy. This time there were no dogs or shadows moving. It was what I didn't see that bothered me. I sensed strongly that something was not right, up ahead. As I got to the spot on the road, I nervously glanced back. A short distance behind me, walking in my direction, was a man. I turned around, thinking he had just walked onto the road from one of the many side paths. Then I remembered a recent story one of the locals had shared about a tourist walking at night in the same area. The tourist was robbed and then killed by a man with a machete.

I turned around to see where the guy was. I was startled to see him right behind me. With one hand he grabbed me by the shirt. With the other he pulled out a machete and held it up to my throat. I was in shock. With the blade to my neck, he pushed me backwards into the bush. Terror grabbed hold of my heart. I thought this was my last moment and that I was going to die. Each second felt like an hour as I was pushed further backwards into the dark cover of the trees.

When he stopped pushing me, a very precious thing happened. This gift of faith began to rise in my heart, and I *knew* the goodness of God. Terror loosened its grip, and I knew God was with me. Whether I lived or died, the Lord would provide.

The man moved in front of me and began taking the few things I had. When he was done, he told me to turn around. Again he placed the machete to my throat and the other hand in the small of my back. With a direct tone, he said, "You may go." As I stepped forward, he removed the blade from my neck. I took a few more steps forward and glanced over my shoulder. He was running away through the trees. God had protected me.

Live With The End in Mind

Getting mugged is one of the best things that has ever happened to me. It made me see life through the eyes of eternity. Not my money, not my clothes, not my personal hopes and dreams, nor any of my accomplishments were of comfort to me, when staring death in the face. All the riches of the world would have been no consolation. The only thing running through my mind was, "Am I right with God? Am I holy?" Nothing else mattered.

We are made for eternity. Our lives are a temporary passing on this earth. Even if we are fortunate to live a hundred years, our earthly lives would only snatch a millionth of a second from eternity. If we lived a thousand years, perhaps half a second of our eternity would be used. Our life is a brief moment in time, a blink of the eye, compared to the eternal life we will live. But what you do in that blink has eternal consequences. Many are living their lives as though they will never die, and in doing so will die and never will have lived. They will have missed their invitation to grow in the life of God and to become holy. The time we have now is schooling for eternity. There is no second chance.

You *will* have a last moment. The time to respond to the grace of God *will* come to an end. It will be the most important day of your life, for the very next moment you will step into eternity.

> Death puts an end to human life as the time open to either accepting or rejecting the divine grace manifested in Christ.[2]

There, you will stand before the judgment of God, and you will be rewarded immediately in accordance with works and faith.[3] Are you living with the end in mind? Jesus said:

> Do not lay up for yourselves treasures on earth, where moth and rust consume and where thieves break in and steal.[4]

If what you treasure can be stolen from you, then it is not worth treasuring. In reality, death will strip us of everything we've earned in our life. All accomplishments, career advancements, positions, popularity, toys, and fancy jewelry are taken from us in that last moment of our lives. Doesn't it seem ridiculous to cling to things we cannot hold, and to live for things that have no eternal value?

Why not spend your life on what will last, instead of what will be taken from you? Jesus said:

> But lay up for yourselves treasures in heaven, where neither moth nor rust consumes and where thieves do not break in and steal.[5]

We lay up treasure in heaven by loving God. This requires placing Jesus at the center of our lives and following in His ways. Jesus said, "If you love me, you will keep my commandments."[6] Obedience has eternal value.

No Time for Others Means No Time for Jesus

Somebody was once asked to spell love. The response was, "T I M E." How you use your time is an indication of what and who you love. Jesus taught, "Truly, I say to you, as you did it to one of the least of these my brethren, you did it to me."[7] Use your time to love Jesus by loving the people around you. Each person you meet is an opportunity to encounter and love Him. It is Jesus that lives within your neighbor. If you don't have time for others, you don't have time for Jesus.

To love or not to love is a choice that impacts eternity. It is the only question that eternally matters. You can only bring two things to heaven: your soul and the souls of others. Let your driving force in life be this and nothing else. To love someone is to desire the highest good for them. The highest good is heaven. We must love people to heaven through words, prayers, and works of love, and by this we love God. Are you making an eternal impact with the time God has given you?

It is within TIME that we respond to the grace of God. In your last moments, will you have wished you had used your time differently? The average person watches four hours of television per day.[8] If you slept an average of eight hours per day, twenty-five percent of your waking life would be spent watching TV. What a waste of the gift of life!

Imagine standing before Jesus the moment after death. He goes through your book and sees one quarter of your waking life was spent gazing at a box. Might He wonder what the love of your life was? I am not saying you shouldn't watch television, but it is of little benefit in working out your salvation. In fact, much of what is aired will harm your soul rather than help it. And if the way you use your time hurts your relationship with Christ, you need to change what you are watching. In the eyes of eternity, it is not worth it. Use your time with the end in mind.

Many people spend their life in pursuit of goals. It is good to have goals, but what fuels your efforts is much more important than the achievements. St. John of the Cross said, "At the evening of life, we shall be judged on our love."[9] The accomplishment of any life goal, even if it is religious in nature, means little without love. When love becomes our only aim, then success or failure, it matters not, because all is surrendered to Jesus. If Jesus allows success, then that is good for a soul that loves. If Jesus allows failure, then that also is good for a soul that loves. If you love God above all else, then nothing can be taken from you, because everything is His.

Spend your time loving God. Dedicate part of your day

to prayer. Nothing is worth doing, unless it is first given to Jesus. God has given you each day; give it back to Him by establishing a prayer life. Every morning I say, "Jesus, I gladly give my life to you today."

We Will Never Regret Growing in Holiness

Attend mass every Sunday, and during the week if possible. St. Peter Julian Eymard said, when speaking of the mass:

> You cannot do anything to glorify God more, nor profit your soul more, than to devoutly assist at (mass), and assist as often as possible.[10]

If you wish to build the kingdom of God, then go to mass. It will be the best use of your time. St. Bernard says:

> One merits more by devoutly assisting at Holy Mass than by distributing all of his goods to the poor and traveling all over the world on pilgrimage.[11]

Through private revelation, the Lord told St. Gertrude:

> You may be sure that regarding one who devoutly assists at Holy Mass, I will send him as many Saints to comfort him and protect him during the last moments of his life as there will have been Masses which he has heard well.[12]

Our goal in life should be sainthood. *This is our potential.* God doesn't just want to save us from sin; He wants us to share in His Divine life, bringing us to heaven. Only saints go to heaven, and we are all called to be saints. To be a saint is God's will for your life. "Heaven is the ultimate end and fulfillment of the deepest human longings."[13] Let nothing distract you from this.

To be a saint, you must be holy. When you are holy, you become Christ-like, and this requires you to discipline your life to practice virtue.

> A virtue is a habitual and firm disposition to do good. It allows the person not only to perform good acts, but to give the best of himself.[14]

The virtuous person practices good that requires human effort. It means to live out "WWJD" ... What would Jesus do? God's grace will help you choose good, but that doesn't mean you are free from sacrifice and struggle. To be a purpose-driven Catholic is to live a virtuous and holy life.

Now Is the Only Moment You Have

Don't wait to grow in holiness. Some may be tempted to depend on the future for this chance. If that is the case, they will never find the opportunity. The future will never come, because it is always one day ahead. All we have is the present. Since it is God's will for you to be holy, He will give you all the graces you need to be faithful to Him today. In this moment, God is drawing you to Himself. He gives you the graces you need for your situation right now.

It is true that God's grace will come to us tomorrow, and it will be another invitation to grow in holiness. But if today is our last, we will be judged on the grace given up to the moment we die, not the grace of tomorrow. See how foolish it would be to depend on tomorrow's grace, since tomorrow may never come.

To live a life of holiness is to live a life without regret. As one progresses in the spiritual life, one grows deeper and deeper in union with Jesus. This is our saving consolation. In your last moment, you will not regret the number of masses you had attended. You will not wish you had prayed less. You won't feel that you had wasted your life caring for and loving your family members. You will regret having been a workaholic. You will feel despair at the thought of unconfessed sin. You will see all worldly accomplishment as dust in the wind.

All Roads Lead to the Same Place

I remember an incident I had driving in rush-hour traffic once. I was in a frantic hurry to get home, but the traffic was going at a snail's pace. My patience was wearing thin. Then, in the midst of the cars honking and weaving in and out of traffic, I was interrupted by a thought: "Where are you rushing to?" I knew immediately this was not only a thought, but the voice of Jesus. I took a moment to watch all the other vehicles around me. Everyone drove as though they had an emergency. I began to wonder where each person was going, as one car turned left and another turned right. And in that moment, I realized each person, including myself, would end up in the same place. All roads lead to the judgment seat of God.

Jesus spoke of two roads a person can walk:

> The gate is wide and the road is easy that leads to
> destruction, and there are many who take it. For
> the gate is narrow and the road is hard that leads
> to life, and there are few who find it.[15]

The easy road is the self-indulgent road where one
devotes his or her life's activities to serving self. The road is
easy because it involves no sacrifice, other than for self-gain. A
life in pursuit of ease is a selfish life.

The hard road is a life of self-denial for the sake of Christ.
It is the desire to submit one's will over to God's. On this road,
one chooses out of love to devote life's activities to obedience
of God. The more one loves his or her own will over God's,
the more the narrow road is difficult and unattractive. As love
for God increases, this road will not seem so difficult, because
when you love somebody you are willing to sacrifice for them.

Is your life focused on getting ahead, accomplishing
your goals, acquiring a big house, nice clothes, and a fancy car?
Are you focused on what you have and what you still have left
to attain? Do you think more about material possessions than
about caring for the souls of those around you? This road has
a very meaningless end.

The road of selfish pursuits and the road of sainthood
both lead to the same place. Both end with the soul bare
before God. One soul finds destruction; the other soul finds
eternal life. The choice is ours as to which one we travel.

❧❧

God created you with the end in mind. *His glory is your potential.* He loves you so much that He desires to spend eternity with you. Are you living with an eternal perspective? You will stand before the Almighty one day. Obedience to Him will be your treasure, and the virtuous life will be your crowning jewel. Spend your life on love, for Love spent His on you.

Chapter Nine

The Catholic Church: God's Idea

You are Peter, and on this rock I will build my church.
❧Matthew 16:18❧

Through countryside and city [the Apostles] preached,
and they appointed their earliest converts,
testing them by the Spirit,
to be the bishops and deacons of future believers.
❧Pope Clement I – 80 A.D.❧

To live in God's full plan is to be in His Church.

My sister-in-law, while teaching her Grade Two class, asked the students which meals that their moms made were their favorites. One of her students replied, "The chicken in the bucket with the man's face on it." I'm sure Colonel Sanders would be smiling.

Where do you eat out most often? Odds are you aren't going to an upscale restaurant to eat a five-course meal prepared by a gourmet chief. You're likely going to a fast food joint, getting your fries delicately sautéed in a deep fryer by a sixteen-year-old kid. One out of every four people in America visits a fast food restaurant in a day.[1] We are seduced by the salty fries, the juicy/greasy hamburgers, and the convenience of the meal. Our life is fast-paced, so we like our meals that way, too. Fast food fits our lifestyle. It is the easy way to go. But just because it's the easiest, doesn't mean it is the most nourishing. A *McDonald's* super-sized Coke, fries, and Big Mac are so packed with calories, you would have to walk seven hours straight to burn them off.[2]

A home-cooked, balanced meal is the healthier choice. I love eating my mom's cooking. Each meal is always balanced, always delicious, and nothing can beat the seasoning of love that goes into each meal.

Which Church to Attend?

Where to go for spiritual nourishment is an important question because it has eternal consequences. There are more denominations than there are fast food joints. Each church serves up a variety of teachings and practices to feed your soul, but each one teaches something a little different. After awhile, you have to begin to wonder: which one gives the best nourishment? Who is right, because they can't all be? What is my guarantee of truth?

I recently spoke with a woman who was looking for a good church to attend. She had participated in many different denominations but couldn't find one that fit her needs. She had been through years of church-jumping but had never found a spiritual home. She was looking for a place to be fed.

Without a clear spiritual authority we become lost, like sheep without a shepherd. We are attracted to the road of least resistance. We go to where the grazing is easy, sticking with the popular opinion. The danger is that popular opinion can be dead wrong. When a teaching of a church becomes challenging and demands a change of lifestyle, it is often ignored, or people look for a new denomination to fit their system of beliefs. They will justify their move, saying, "God has led me to another church." This usually happens because the church they left did not correspond with their set of beliefs, or their "feeling" of being spiritually fed went unmet. But have you ever believed something that was incorrect, even though it felt really true? We all have.

Because you accept something to be true doesn't mean it is true. I used to believe in Santa Claus. He used to give me presents every Christmas. Later I found out that Santa Claus was Uncle Albert! The consequence of this misconception was minimal, but not so with our belief in God. Our eternity is at stake.

Some people believe, that "if you confess with your lips that Jesus is Lord and believe in your heart that God raised him from the dead, you will be saved" [3] (Romans 10:9). Others claim the works of looking after the hungry, thirsty, naked, sick and imprisoned, puts them in the group of either the saved or non-saved (Matthew 33:31-46). There is no mention of confessing anything with the lips in Matthew 33. It is all about the works that you do. Still others believe in their ability to interpret the Bible correctly, because the Holy Spirit "will guide you into all the truth" [4] (John 16:13) and that scripture alone will show the way to eternal life. Still others feel that confessing sin to a priest is not necessary, because "who can forgive sins but God alone?" [5] (Mark 2:7), or that the Eucharist is just a symbol, since "it is the spirit that gives life, the flesh is of no avail" [6] (John 6:63). The reasons for our beliefs can seem so confusing and contradictory. Just because we can use a scripture verse that seems to support what we believe, it does not mean we have interpreted that scripture correctly or considered its context properly.

There are many well-intentioned pastors who give

great sermons, passionately believing their interpretation of scripture is right, while another pastor down the road firmly believes in a conflicting interpretation of scripture. They both believe that the Holy Spirit has inspired them with an insight superior to the other. Obviously this doesn't work. The result is thousands of different Christian denominations teaching different things, each one believing their way is the truth. Good intentions do not guarantee sound doctrine! You only have to look at the thousands of different denominations to know this is true.

There are some who would argue it doesn't matter if there are many different denominations and different interpretations of scripture. They would say that as long as we have core beliefs in common, or that you believe in Jesus, that this is all God cares about. They argue that the differences between denominations are manmade and not important in the "Big Picture." Really? If that is your doctrine, then I challenge you to back it up with scripture! Do you really think that Jesus intended for many different denominations? Or that it doesn't matter? Or that the Bible is all you need? *If so, back it up with scripture!* Back it up with something other than opinion, because opinions don't carry you into heaven. Opinions can be dead wrong and have devastating eternal consequences.

We Need Divine Guidance and a Guarantee of Truth

If Jesus were to select a church for you to attend, which one would He choose? The answer is simple: the one He established; the one described all over in scripture; and the one He promised to lead in the fullness of truth. Jesus said, "And I tell you, you are Peter, and on this rock I will build my church."[7] Where is the church that Jesus established? Look to the Vatican, and you'll find your answer. It is here that Jesus' commands to teach (Matthew 28:20) and feed (John 2:17) all nations are being fulfilled, and it is all seasoned in love.

The Catholic Church can trace its roots back to Jesus and the Apostles. Every single other church has its beginnings here. Trace any denomination back through history, and you find the same starting point.

> The Pentecostal churches, for example, are nineteenth-century offshoots of the Holiness churches, which were offshoots of the Methodist Church, which was an offshoot of the Anglican Church, which was a sixteenth-century offshoot of the Catholic Church.[8]

You can also be sure that if Jesus began something, He will see to completion what He has started. The Apostles' ministry was a continuation of Jesus' ministry.[9] He shared with them His authority to teach and to lead people in truth. Jesus said to the Twelve, "He who receives you receives me, and he who receives me receives him who sent me."[10] The bishops of the world are the successors of the Apostles, and they continue to carry out Jesus' mission, in union with Peter's successor, our Pope.

One of the most important teachings in the Catholic faith is that it has protection from doctrinal error. When the Bishops of the world, in unity with the successor of Peter, make an official statement on faith and morals, it can be trusted to be true. Jesus assured the Church of this when He told the Apostles, "I am with you always, to the close of the age."[11] He promised the Holy Spirit to guide them in all truth.[12] Individuals can be wrong, even bishops can be misled, but the successors of the Apostles cannot be wrong when they speak in union with the Pope on matters of faith and morals.

Your Eternal Soul Is Safe with the Catholic Church

Jesus conferred a share of His infallibility to the Church in order to preserve her purity of faith.[13] As it was impossible for Jesus to be in error, it is impossible for the Church to be in error when concerning faith and morals. We can trust our eternal soul to the teaching authority of the Catholic Church because it is Christ who teaches us through her. This knowledge should fill you with tremendous peace. With all the choices of churches out there, teaching different things, you know there is one Church that you can depend on to be true.

The Catholic position on teaching authority can appear very arrogant at a glance. After all, who claims to be free from error? We must remember that it was Jesus who placed the Church in this position, not man. Jesus spoke to Peter and said:

> I will give you the keys of the kingdom of heaven, and whatever you bind on earth shall be bound in heaven, and whatever you loose on earth shall be loosed in heaven.[14]

Since Jesus guarantees Peter that whatever he binds

and looses on earth shall be done identically in heaven, we can assume Peter's binding and loosing will be without error. God would not bind or loose something that is contrary to His will. God cannot lie, nor can He make a mistake, so placing Himself in agreement with Peter's actions have to mean Peter's binding and loosing will be without error. The infallibility of the Catholic Church means that God Himself will divinely lead His Church in truth in the areas of faith and morals, through the earthly authorities He has established.

Infallibility Was Jesus' Idea

The Catholic Church has always understood herself to have received the teaching infallibility of Christ. The Church believes this because this is the truth the Apostles were taught from Jesus. The Apostles in turn passed this teaching onto their successors. Never was this teaching invented. It always existed in the early Church, beginning with the Apostles, and continues to this day. The infallibility of the Catholic Church is real, and it comes from the promises of Jesus Himself.

Jesus knew that the salvation of man would be determined by the clear communication of truth. It is no wonder Jesus commanded His Apostles to teach others to observe all that He had commanded.[15] False teaching could lead to eternal ruin. It makes logical sense for Jesus to establish a sure way of leading His people in truth. His priority would be to make certain His teachings would be clearly understood. To leave your people prayerfully guessing, trying to understand matters of faith and the meaning of scripture on their own, would be devastating. The result would be a variety of different views on the same line of scripture.

Take, for example, the Last Supper, when Jesus picked

up a piece of bread and said, "Take, eat; this is my body."[16] Some might say He meant it figuratively, but what did the Apostles believe Jesus meant? They were the ones present when He said those words, so their understanding would be the most accurate. One only has to look at the teachings of the Apostles' direct successors to understand Jesus' teaching on the Eucharist. Every single early Church Father believed that when Jesus said "this is my body," He meant it was literally His flesh. They believed this because this is what was taught by the Apostles, who were taught by Jesus. The Catholic Church has always maintained this position throughout the last two thousand years. As a Catholic, you do not have to wonder what Jesus' words meant, because Jesus teaches us through the Tradition and teaching authority of His Church.

Scripture Does Not Self-Interpret

Other Christian churches reject the Catholic Church's teaching authority and her Tradition, claiming that the Bible alone is our spiritual authority. This teaching is called *sola scriptura*. It is the notion that scripture is all that is needed in proposing what is to be believed in the Christian faith. An individual is left with the responsibility for interpreting scripture for themselves. Obviously this leads to problems with interpretation, since one person will see scripture very differently than another. *Sola Scriptura* is not a fulfillment of Jesus' promise to lead us into all truth, because there can only be one truth and not many different ones.[17]

Sola scriptura leads one to believe that if it can't be found in scripture then it is a manmade tradition and not a doctrine guided by the Holy Spirit. What they fail to realize is that *sola scriptura* is unscriptural. Nowhere in the Bible does it say that scripture is the sole authority for the Christian life. There are verses that point to the usefulness of scripture, such as 2 Timothy 3:16, which says, "All scripture is inspired by God and profitable for teaching, for reproof, for correction, and for training in righteousness."[18] However the Bible does not support scripture as the sole authority in the Christian life. The teaching of *sola scriptura* is therefore unscriptural and is a false doctrine.

Apostolic Tradition Is in the Bible

According to the Bible, scripture is not the sole rule of faith for a Christian. We must also examine apostolic tradition, that is the teachings of the Apostles and their successors, when determining what is truth. This is the biblical view of teaching authority.

The Bible contains many references of this tradition. St. Paul wrote, "I commend you because you remember me in everything and maintain the traditions even as I have delivered them to you."[19] Again he writes to the Thessalonians, "So then, brethren, stand firm and hold to the traditions which you were taught by us, either by word of mouth or by letter."[20] St. Paul even warns the Thessalonians to stay away from those who did not follow the traditions that were taught:

> Now we command you, brethren, in the name of our Lord Jesus Christ, that you keep away from any brother who is living in idleness and not in accord with the tradition that you received from us.[21]

The traditions of the Apostles and their office were passed onto successors. This is called apostolic succession. St. Paul highlights the importance of this succession by saying to Timothy, "What you have heard from me before many witnesses entrust to faithful men who will be able to teach others also."[22]

In the beginning of the Church, there was no written New Testament. Therefore it was never the plan of Jesus for His followers to base their faith on just the written word. Living by scripture alone would have been impossible. Teachings were passed on from the Apostles to their successors orally. St. Paul demonstrates this by saying to the Corinthian Church, "For I delivered to you as of first importance what I also received, that Christ died for our sins according to the Scriptures."[23] What gives St. Paul's his teaching authority is the fact that he *received* his teaching from tradition. This is his assurance to the people that he didn't make it up.

Is the teaching you are receiving coming from the successors of the Apostles? If not what is your reassurance that it is correct? As a Catholic, my heart is at peace knowing that I can trust what the Catholic Church teaches, because it is coming out of apostolic succession.

If you Trust the Scriptures, Why Not Trust the Church Who Gave Them to You?

The Catholic Church has demonstrated its infallibility right from the beginning of Christianity. An example of this is the formation of the Bible. Much of the New Testament scriptures are the oral tradition of the Catholic Church written down. It took centuries before the Church decided which books would be included in the Bible. There were many writings being used in the early Church. Through time the Catholic Church, guided by the Holy Spirit, determined which writings were without error and collected these writings to form the New Testament.

If we trust the infallibility of scripture, by default we trust the infallible decisions that the Catholic Church made when putting together the New Testament scriptures. To a non-Catholic I would say, *"Consider placing your trust in the Church who gave you the scriptures you trust."* Please re-read that last sentence.

Wouldn't the Church who prayerfully decided which books would be part of the Bible also have the most accurate understanding of them? It was the original historical, cultural, and theological understandings of these scriptures' passages that determined whether or not they would be included in the New Testament. The Church who discerned the content of the Bible is in the best position to discern its meaning.

We cannot claim to have the fullness of truth without acknowledging *both scripture and tradition* as the means by which Jesus has established His Church. When we reject the teachings of the Catholic Church, we are ignoring the teachings that are rooted in the teachings of Christ and the Apostles.

It is God's will for all humanity to be in communion with His Church. Jesus prayed:

> I ask not only on behalf of these, but also on behalf of those who will believe in me through their word, that they may all be one. As you, Father, are in me and I am in you, may they also

be in us, so that the world may believe that you have sent me ... so that they may be one, as we are one.[24]

Jesus desired that His Church be united in the same way as He is united to the Father. He wants unity, but unity does not come at the expense of changing teachings to fit other beliefs. Jesus said, "He who hears you hears me, and he who rejects you rejects me."[25] When we accept the Catholic Church and her teachings we are accepting the fullness of Christ's plan for our lives.

Every doctrine and discipline of the Catholic Church is focused on helping you to grow in holiness. Jesus desires that you be holy. He desires that you would become a saint. Therefore, all the laws and teachings of His Church can be trusted to help you grow in His Divine life. Take responsibility for your faith. Study the *Catechism of the Catholic Church* and the *Compendium,* which is a summary of the Catechism. Get your hands on the encyclicals of Popes. If you struggle with certain teachings of the Church, find out why the Church teaches what it does on the subject. There is a reason, and it is always for your benefit and holiness. Tradition, scripture, and the Church's teaching authority are God's means of communicating His truth to you.

Complete Understanding Isn't Necessary to Trust

You don't have to understand all the Church's teachings to be in communion with the Church, but you do have to accept them. For example, it is impossible to fully understand teachings on the incarnation or the Eucharist. They remain a mystery to us, but we do not need to fully understand these truths to trust they are true.

୨ஜ

Since the fullness of truth is within the Catholic Church, the fullness of God's purpose for your life is there as well. To live in God's full plan is to embrace His Church: the Catholic Church. It is the visible plan of God's personal love for you and for all humanity.[26] "Only through this Church can one obtain the fullness of the means of salvation."[27] The Catholic Church is your spiritual home, seasoned with love. It is your protection against error and offers you the full purpose of God's will for your life. The Catholic Church is God's will for you.

Chapter Ten

Touching The Wood

Apart from the cross,
there is no other ladder
by which we may get to heaven.
෴ St. Rosa de Lima ෴

If any man would come after me,
let him deny himself and take up his cross
daily and follow me.
෴ Luke 9:23 ෴

Imagine having the opportunity to touch the actual cross of Jesus. What an honor that would be, to embrace the wood upon which hung the savior of the world. A man named Simon had this opportunity, but it seems that he did not count it as a blessing. The event happened during the passion of Christ.

> As they led [Jesus] away, they seized a man, Simon of Cyrene, who was coming from the country, and they laid the cross on him, and made him carry it behind Jesus.[1]

Simon did not go willingly. He was seized and forced to do something he did not want to do. This was more than an inconvenience, but a share in the humiliation of a condemned criminal! Little did Simon know, this was also a share in a glory to come.

For eternity all of heaven will remember that cross and the blood of Jesus spilt on it. Billions of voices will be raised in an eternal song of adoration because of what happened on that wood. Every angel in heaven that day would have loved to have traded places with Simon, but it was Simon, ordained by God, who was given this precious blessing to participate with Jesus in the redemption of the world. If Simon had known the significance of what was happening, do you think the soldiers would have had to force him to carry the cross? Had he known, I'm guessing he would have been a lot more willing.

The reality is, we are often like Simon, when it comes to suffering, and fail to see the significance of these moments. Our suffering can be redemptive. Through every trial, suffering, and inconvenience allowed in our lives, God invites us to unite these with Jesus' suffering, for the redemption of the world. Each struggle that we face is an invitation to touch the cross of Jesus and impact eternity.

The angels continue to stand in awe of this, because we can do something they cannot. In fact, St Pio da Pietrelcina, more affectionately known to many as Padre Pio, said this: "The angels envy us for one thing only; they cannot suffer for God."[2] *We* can touch the cross of Jesus through our suffering. *We* can receive the gift of redemptive suffering.

How Well Do You Suffer?

The question is not *if* we will suffer, but *how* we suffer. Trials are unavoidable, but to despair in them is not. If our response to hardship is to blame God or others, we will become bitter. Bitter people often fight against circumstances beyond their control and become unable to find any substantial meaning to their hardships. They may say, "I am a stronger person because of it," but if their faith in God has not increased, or if their suffering was not offered up for others, it was wasted suffering.

Some may see God as the source of their distress. They feel He is unwilling to help in their trouble, and their trust in Him begins to erode. This belief forces one to trust in oneself for the solution rather than God, because God is believed to be absent from the situation. When in this position, trials are overwhelming; a person is anxious about much, and their suffering is purposeless.

It is always possible to find meaning in suffering. It is not God's will for us to despair in our crosses. We will not have full knowledge, as God does, as to why certain things are allowed, but this should not prevent us from finding purpose in our trials.

Understanding redemptive suffering can give eternal meaning to every cross in life. All that Jesus is, He shares with you. As He offered His passion for the accomplishment of the Father's will, you can do the same in Christ as a member of His Body. Your sufferings can become avenues of grace, offered on behalf of others or for personal intentions, for the accomplishment of God's will.

The key is to make a decision of faith to unite your hardships to the passion of Christ. This makes suffering redemptive, because it is connected to the redemptive suffering of Jesus. We are part of the Body of Christ and can participate in His redeeming role. Spiritually speaking, we touch the cross of Jesus. We can be like Simon of Cyrene, following Jesus, participating in the passion of Christ for the salvation of souls.

St. Paul knew the power of redemptive suffering. He

said, "Now I rejoice in my sufferings for your sake, and in my flesh I complete what is lacking in Christ's afflictions for the sake of his body, that is, the church."[3] St. Paul brought about a greater good through his personal trials. He found purpose in his afflictions by offering them for other Christians. In this, he said he rejoiced!

Later, while in jail for preaching the gospel, he writes to the Ephesians, "So I ask you not to lose heart over what I am suffering for you, which is your glory."[4] Many would despair at the thought of being unjustly accused and imprisoned. Paul's reputation was destroyed. And can you imagine the rumors floating around about him? Saul, a learned and devout Jew, in jail! It was front page news and great material for the gossip columns. I'm sure the neighbors were talking, if not the whole town. But no despairing or complaining word comes from his lips, nor any thought of revenge mentioned. In fact, St. Paul considers his jail time as a means to obtaining *glory* for the Christians to whom he wrote. This was not a defeat but an opportunity to gain victory.

Suffering, United to the Cross, Equals Grace

Maybe you haven't experienced wrongful imprisonment like St. Paul, but how about a jail sentence of another kind? The unfair judgments of others, rumors damaging reputations, and jealous, deliberate lies tainting one's name: these are the prison cells of many. Your cell may not consist of bars and chains but of rejection by others. Scripture says:

> Beloved, do not be surprised at the fiery ordeal which comes upon you to prove you, as though something strange were happening to you. But

> rejoice in so far as you share Christ's sufferings,
> that you may also rejoice and be glad when his
> glory is revealed.[5]

We should never assume that if we having suffering in our lives we are outside of God's purpose. On the contrary, it is these sufferings that bring about His purposes.

The graces of baptism allow us to offer our trials in union with Christ. In the Old Testament, one role of the priest was to offer sacrifices on behalf of the sins committed by God's people. In the New Testament, Jesus is both high priest and the sacrifice. He offers Himself as the atoning sacrifice for sin. Since we are baptized into Christ, we share in His priesthood.[6] This share is called the *common priesthood of the faithful*. Through the grace of baptism, we can offer our lives, both the joys and sorrows, in union with Christ, for the redemption of mankind. St. Paul urged the Romans:

> I appeal to you therefore, brothers and sisters,
> by the mercies of God, to present your bodies
> as a living sacrifice, holy and acceptable to God,
> which is your spiritual worship.[7]

The problem with us being a living sacrifice is that we often kick and scream when things get tough. Jesus offers us the perfect model for handling life's crosses. As His passion was about to begin, He said, "Father, if you are willing, remove this cup from me; yet, not my will but yours be done."[8] Jesus' first response was to ask the Father to remove the suffering, but He remained firm to accept His Father's will. There was no complaining, only perfect submission and trust in the Father. The offering of Jesus' life opened the way of grace for mankind.

This should be our response as well, and the result will be grace for the Body of Christ.

Suffering, united to the cross of Jesus, equals grace. All the suffering in your life right now can bring about tremendous glory for God. From the small inconveniences of the day, to sicknesses or diseases, to the pain of losing a loved one, all suffering is an opportunity for grace. You don't have to be a world-renowned preacher to win souls for Christ. You just need to be a faithful soul who lovingly offers every trial and woe for the conversion of hearts. You can do this. In fact, God is calling you to do this. You can gain immense grace for those you love by offering all that you are for them. This is nothing less than the way of Christ. His whole life was an offering to the Father, and He shares this role with you. Aren't we to be Christ-like? Offer your crosses then, as Jesus did, for the will of God.

God Has a Purpose for Everyday

Everything that happens to you has an eternal meaning. In the eyes of God, every day is a day of purpose. Each moment is an opportunity to impact eternity. Life's trials aren't allowed so that we can perfect the art of complaining. They are permitted always for a greater unseen purpose. Be thankful for what trials are allowed now, because you won't always have the opportunity to offer it up later. The saints in heaven can't do what you have a chance to do: offer sufferings for God's greater glory. There isn't any suffering in heaven. Now is your only opportunity, for you aren't promised tomorrow. Therefore, make use of what God has given today, for tomorrow may never come.

St. Paul, living with an eternal perspective, said, "I consider that the sufferings of this present time are not worth comparing with the glory that is to be revealed to us."[9] A soul that suffers in love, suffers only temporarily in anticipation of the glory of God. Eternal union with Him is our hope, not the temporary ease of this life. If we grumble about our trials, our hope is in this world and not in Christ. If we fully knew the eternal happiness that God desires to share with us, our momentary hardship would be gladly offered to Him.

Find Your Cross in Your Complaints

We must offer our crosses instead of complaining about trials. Philippians 3:10 says, "That I may know [Christ] and the power of his resurrection, and may share his sufferings, becoming like him in his death."[10] I don't know about you, but I'm much more excited to know Christ and the power of His resurrection than to share His suffering! I definitely don't feel like being crucified to become like Him in His death. I am thankful God knows my selfishness. He knows my weakness of faith. Therefore, the crosses He allows are in His perfect timing and in perfect size.

What are the crosses God is asking you to unite to Him? The big ones are often easy to see, but it is the little ones that can make you a saint. Do you realize in your complaining you'll find your cross? Once you realize this, they are easy to find. Our aggravations and the pet peeves during the day are crosses to offer to Christ. Complaining brings no good. In fact, you'll miss the grace because you gripe. Every complaining word is a missed opportunity to love. Stop complaining and start offering, lest the grace of God pass you by. Remember, in your complaint you will find your cross.

Believe that when you offer your suffering to Christ, grace is beginning to flow into the intention for which you offered it.

Visit the Niagara Falls and you'll feel the thunder of more than two million liters of water falling 792 meters every second.[11] The power and volume cascading down is incredible. If you wished to take some of the Niagara Falls back home, you would be limited, not by the amount of water flowing over the falls, but by the container used to catch the water. If you bring a shot glass, you would get one ounce. If you bring a ten-gallon barrel, you would get ten gallons. If you bring a swimming pool to catch the water, then you would get a swimming pool full of water. Just as the container extended under the Niagara Falls determines the amount of water caught, so too, does our faith determine the amount of redeeming grace actualized in our suffering.

We must make a decision of the will to unite our suffering with the cross of Jesus. Believe that great falls of grace will flow into the intention for which you offer your suffering. If you do not, your suffering is wasted! How much grace is lost when complaining about the things over which we have no control? It is ironic that the things we cannot change just may change if we offer our frustrations up for the will of God the Father.

Selfishness Is Exposed in Suffering

Your cross is an opportunity to love. Often when we are in pain we become very self-centered. The last thing we are thinking about is helping others. Selfishness is exposed in suffering. Our needs come to the forefront, and others take a back seat. Obviously, this was not the way of Jesus. Even when on the cross, He suffered selflessly. Jesus loved the good thief and said, "Truly, I say to you, today you will be with me in Paradise;"[12] as the soldiers divided His clothes and the rulers scoffed at Him, He cried out, "Father forgive them; for they know not what they do;"[13] and He ensured the care of Mary, His mother, to the apostle, John, saying, "'Behold, your mother!' And from that hour the disciple took her to his own home."[14]

The enemy of redemptive suffering is selfishness. Self-centered suffering only intensifies anguish. The more we love ourselves above God, the more overwhelming the cross. The more we love God above ourselves, the more meaningful and joyous our cross will be. When love becomes our motivation then we can "endure all things."[15] The more we love, the less it will hurt to bear the cross. Mother Teresa said, "I have found the paradox that if I love until it hurts, then there is no hurt, but only more love."[16] Only a selfless heart experiences this truth.

Some may gasp and say, "But you don't know what I am going through." You are right, but God does. He is the only One that will give meaning to your cross. If it seems an impossibility to suffer selflessly for the sake of His will, this is very good. God has opened your eyes to your need for Him. You cannot do it on your own. Ask Jesus to give you His heart of love. God will allow us to be in impossible positions so that we would turn to Him in faith. Acknowledging our helplessness before God allows Him to help us. Be encouraged by Jesus' words, "With men this is impossible, but with God all things are possible."

All Suffering Can Be Life-Giving

My mother had seven kids; she said my sister, Kathleen, had the biggest head. It was a sacrifice on her body to give birth each time, but in each cross life was brought forth. The rewards of labor pains are far outweighed by the blessing of family. Consider your cross as spiritual birth pains giving God's life. In Romans it says:

> We know that the whole creation has been groaning in labour pains until now; and not only the creation, but we ourselves, who have the first fruits of the Spirit, groan inwardly while we wait for adoption, the redemption of our bodies.[17]

❧❧

Your suffering can be life-giving when centered on Christ or life-taking when centered on self. You may not choose your cross, but you can choose how to carry it.

Chapter Eleven

Trials Of Faith

We always find that those who walked closest to Christ were those who had to bear the greatest trials.
❧ *St. Teresa of Avila* ❧

One February, my brother Keith and his new girlfriend (now wife) Janelle came over for a visit. I had met this young lady on a few occasions before and had seen their relationship grow to become quite a committed one over a matter of a few months. During the conversation, Janelle suggested with excitement that Keith show me what he had given her for Valentine's Day. After a little prodding, he cheerfully agreed and went to his bag and pulled out a small gift box. He carefully opened the box and removed from it a small white vase, its contents concealed by soft white paper. Keith began to delicately peel away the white paper, revealing the treasured Valentine's gift: a black, dull stone.

"You got her a rock for Valentine's Day?" I asked in disbelief.

"It's a not a rock," Keith responded. "It's a piece of coal."

"You got Janelle a lump of coal for Valentine's Day! What kind of stupid gift is that?" I said sarcastically. I couldn't believe what I was hearing. I was sure he was in the dog house for this one.

"Obviously, you don't know anything about coal," Keith said confidently. "You see, sometimes when coal is in the ground, the earth acts against it with tremendous force. After enough time, heat and pressure, the lump of coal in the ground is transformed into a beautiful, shining diamond." Keith was smiling as Janelle's eyes twinkled.

He continued in a rather droll way, "You see, this piece of coal represents our future, and what is to come."

Keith was pretty smooth I must say, because I don't think anybody else could have pulled off giving a discarded lump of coal as a romantic Valentine's gift. This event, however, made me think of how God allows our faith to be pressed so we will shine.

For Faith to Grow it Must Be Tried

We can live a Christian lifestyle, yet be so self-reliant that we have very little need for faith. We may be going to church, living a moral life, even praying regularly, but active trust in God may be non-existent. There is no desperation, no seeking His guidance, no awareness of helplessness without God. With a tendency for selfishness within our hearts, we take the road of least resistance, and this road requires little faith. It is much harder to exercise faith in a normal stress-free day, because we tend not to ask for help from God when things are easy. In truth, we need God in every moment of the day, and often it is trials that awaken us to this reality.

God will purify the areas of our faith which exclude Him. Like coal under pressure, that which we trust crumbles and is purified under the hand of God. Sometimes He does this by allowing what we have faith in to disappoint us in times of trial. *Disappointment is an indication of misplaced faith.* When trusting our talents, He will allow complete failure. When having faith in appearances, He will cause dissatisfaction with looks. When trusting the intellect, reason will fail to bring a solution to the problem. When relying on feelings, God brings dry spells so there is no more emotional consolation.

When our faith is in others rather than God, He will allow us to be disappointed by them or remove them from our lives. Either way, our reliance on them is broken. This will even happen with people in spiritual authority over us, or ministries with which we are involved. Our supports of faith should not be what we have faith in. If we trust in the blessing of God more than in Him who blesses, He will eventually remove the blessing.

This purification of faith is God's love in action, because He alone brings salvation. We need to recognize we are nothing without Him. To have faith in good things does nothing for our soul. It is necessary to entrust ourselves to the source of all goodness, which is God Himself, and not place our faith in the good things He has made. After enough time and pressure, our misplaced faith will crumble, and all that we will have left is God. What a beautiful place this is, for here faith shines like a diamond before Him. It can withstand much weight because impurities are gone, and beautiful is its ability to reflect the light of Christ.

Faith relies in God's providence, and must be tested for it to grow. We often admire people of great faith, wishing we were like them. Modern-day saints, such as Mother Teresa and Pope John Paul II, are inspiring examples for the world to follow. But we can fall into the temptation of romanticizing their faith if we look at them with a quick glance. We want their trust in God, but we would likely reconsider if faced with the trials that had allowed their faith to increase. Our selfishness desires easy faith, but this kind does not exist.

Abraham is the father of our faith, and he experienced many trials. In Genesis 12:1, God called to him, saying, "[Abram], go from your country and your kindred and your father's house to the land that I will show you."[1] It sounds like a wonderful promise, but it required much trust. Abraham had to uproot himself, his wife, his nephew, his possessions, his cattle, his hired help, and his slaves to go a foreign land, leaving all that was familiar. Notice that God didn't give an address. He just said go. Nor did He say how or when He would deliver on the promise. Yet Abraham didn't question. Realize this happened when Abraham was seventy-five years old! Now I'm not seventy-five, but at that age I'd be thinking more about my pension than starting a new career. My prayer to God would be, "Better show me now, 'cause I don't have many years left." Abraham's obedience was faith in action. God delivered on His promise, giving them the land of Canaan. As a result, Abraham's trust in the Lord grew.

It goes without exception that those past saints, who had great faith, had to endure great trials. If you are facing a crisis in your life, be encouraged; you are in wonderful company. You are also greatly loved! You are surrounded by a cloud of witnesses who understand trials. Call upon their intercession. Their prayers will assist you. Do not become discouraged. God is not punishing you; He is loving you. This is how God treats those He loves. He draws them to Himself through trials, so they're left with nothing but Him. It is God alone who gives meaning to our lives, and without faith we cannot grow in a relationship with Him.

God's Apparent Absence is His Loving Presence

One means that God uses to try our faith is spiritual dryness. Through stripping us of consolation, He purifies our faith, in order that we trust in Him alone and not our feelings of Him. There will be times in our spiritual life, normally after a conversion or renewal of faith, when God's presence is very tangible. Initially one experiences a "honeymoon" phase, where everything seems wonderful. It is easy to pray; scripture comes alive; and the mass is invigorating. These times of consolation can also come and go throughout one's spiritual life. Often a person can fall into the temptation of seeking the blessings and gifts of God, rather than seeking God, Himself. One may even love the blessing more than He who blesses. Faith at this stage remains very shallow and at an emotional level. Then all of a sudden God allows a crisis of faith. It no longer feels good to follow Jesus. Sometimes we think that because we don't *feel* God's presence, we must be far from Him. This is a deceptive lie. God's apparent absence *is* His loving presence.

Spiritual dryness can be God's action in our lives! He has not left us, but has put His hand upon us. He has not abandoned us, but drawn us closer to Himself. Because He loves us, He doesn't want us to place our faith in the feeling of consolation, because for Him alone is why we have been made. The blessings of God are not God. Spiritual dryness gives us an opportunity for our faith to grow and protects us from loving God's consolations more than loving God.

Trials Are Opportunities for Faith to Grow

God desires to give you much faith. It will not grow within you magically, or through an intellectual study, but through the cross. You will feel threatened and exposed. Your securities will be broken, and life will seem out of control. Be encouraged at this time, for God has not abandoned you. His hand is upon you, taking away that which separates you from Him. He allows trials to bring you to a place of nakedness, where all that you have left is Him. It is at these times that God is vulnerable before you as well. Even when you are left with nothing but Him, you still do not have to choose Him. Some choose to retreat into themselves, allowing their faith to erode. How this must pain God's heart.

One very hot summer's day, when my youngest brother Chris was three years old, our family was out, having one of our regular visits with my great aunt down the street. She has a big yard with many trees, great for playing outside, as well as a big deck, wonderful for entertaining. On this day, the game was "hide and go seek." I don't remember if Chris was hiding or seeking, but he was running as fast as his little legs could go. He ripped around the corner of the house, tripped on the edge of the deck, and fell, face-down, landing hard on the edge of a step, splitting his chin wide open. The gash was too big and too deep for a bandage. My mom rushed her bleeding son to the hospital. The doctors determined it was necessary to stitch the wound, but there was no way they could keep my three-year-old brother from thrashing around in pain. In order to hold down Chris, they wrapped his little body up in a restraining cloth.

My mom recalls the sweltering heat in the town hospital room where her three-year-old son lay, wrapped up and unable to move, his complexion, pale, droplets of sweat forming beads on his face. The doctor's left hand braced Chris' head down. The other hand, holding a needle and thread, moved to the wound; the gash across the chin had to be stitched.

It must have been a terrible experience for Chris, although he doesn't remember it. He was bleeding profusely, confined by the restraints, suffocating in the heat, and had a stranger poking at the gash, causing even more pain. I'm sure his three-year-old mind didn't understand that the restraints were for his protection and the stitching, although painful, would bring healing. How, too, it must have hurt my mom to see her little boy suffer.

God's Silence is His Encouraging Word

When experiencing a trial, have you ever thought, "Why me, God?" The weight of the world presses us down so hard it seems there is nothing we can do. We lay helpless and defenseless, while life pokes at us where it hurts the most. We feel alone, abandoned, and misunderstood. The ordeals of life feel suffocating. We may cry out, "God where are you?" We receive no consolation and believe God has fallen asleep. We don't realize that our restraints are the arms of the heavenly Father. The obvious lack of His presence is His touch. God's silence is His encouraging word, leading us to faith. "For it is the LORD your God who goes with you; he will not fail you or forsake you."[2] He looks into our eyes and says, "You don't understand why, but *good* will come from this."

When God Doesn't Make Sense

What a risk God takes when we don't understand, because we could turn away from Him at any moment. It has happened before. Jesus said, "The bread which I shall give for the life of the world is my flesh."[3] The Jews understood that Jesus meant His literal flesh, because they disputed among themselves saying, "How can this man give us his flesh to eat?"[4] Note that Jesus did not correct them by saying He was only speaking figuratively. This would have been the loving thing to do if they had indeed misinterpreted His words. Instead, Jesus continued to say, "For my flesh is food indeed, and my blood is drink indeed."[5] This statement caused a crisis of faith. Many could not understand or accept this teaching. Their faith was tried, and some turned away. "After this many of his disciples drew back and no longer went about with him."[6] Their religious minds were challenged, and when it did not make sense, they rejected Jesus. They chose to have faith in their own understanding rather than the teaching of Jesus. How this must have pained Jesus' heart.

Jesus wished to give them His very self, yet some would not receive Him. He then turned to His Apostles, testing their faith asking, "Do you also wish to go away?"[7] Jesus needed His Apostles to accept this teaching if they were going to follow Him. It wasn't an option. If they were to stay, they would have to make a choice and trust. If not, the door was open and they were free to leave Him, as did many in the crowd.

Have you ever felt like giving up on God and leaving with the crowd? I am sure the Apostles did. Jesus' teaching on the Eucharist was a great trial of their faith. If I had been one of them, I would have been wondering, "How on earth is Jesus going to give me His flesh to eat?" The Last Supper, where Jesus instituted the Eucharist, had not yet happened. Furthermore, Jesus offered no explanation on exactly how He would pull this off. This was not a consoling time for the Twelve. They had left family, friends, and businesses to follow Jesus, and now He was demanding the ridiculous. They had to accept they were to eat His flesh, or they would have to leave Him.

When circumstances don't make sense, when life gets complicated, and the heart feels it is no longer logical to trust, God is vulnerable before you. It is in these times Jesus would ask you with lovely tenderness, "Do you also wish to go away?" His question exposes God's deepest longing ... to give Himself to you.

Imagine the scene. Jesus asks the Twelve, "Do you also wish to go away?" It becomes dead silent. The Apostles look down, shuffling their feet, some considering their options. They hear some other disciples leaving. Jesus waits. Simon Peter breaks the silence and answers on behalf of the future bishops:

> Lord, to whom shall we go? You have the words
> of eternal life; and we have believed, and have
> come to know, that you are the Holy One of
> God.[8]

At this point, Peter could *not* have figured out how they were going to eat Jesus' flesh. His intellect would not have comprehended the depth of Jesus' teaching, since it had not been fully revealed, but his faith was stronger than his understanding. What Peter had was faith in the One who had taught him, which led him to accept Jesus' words, no matter how controversial they were.

Faith Shines Only in a Cloud of Darkness

God does not owe us an explanation when trials get difficult and sufferings don't make sense. If we did understand as He does, we would have no need for faith. In Hebrews it says, "Without faith it is impossible to please him."[9] Faith shines only when in a cloud of darkness. How His heart delights in us when we trust without understanding. This is the childlike faith God wants us to have. Jesus said, "Truly, I say to you, unless you turn and become like children, you will never enter the kingdom of heaven."[10] A child does not fully understand the things of the adult world, yet a child trusts his parents.

If we understand fully our trials, we have no need of God. It was Adam and Eve's prideful desire for knowledge to be like God that motivated them to disobey Him. The serpent tempted them with the fruit of the tree, saying:

> "For God knows that when you eat of it your eyes will be opened, and you will be like God, *knowing* good and evil." So when the woman saw ... that the tree was to be *desired to make one wise,* she took of its fruit and ate; and she also gave some to her husband, and he ate [emphasis added].[11]

Adam and Eve sought knowledge that had not been given to them by God. Their desire to be like God removed the necessity to entrust themselves to Him. After all, if you gain all the wisdom of your Creator, knowing all He knows, why would you need Him? God allows your understanding to fail you, so that you can trust in His unfailing love.

The uncertain future is also a trial of faith. If fear rises in our heart, it is because our trust in God is weak. It is as though we are saying to our heavenly Father, "You will not provide for me." People ask: What is God's will for my life? Who does He want me to marry? How many kids should I have? Where does He want me to live? What kind of job should I get? What is my vocation? If God answered these questions today, we would have no need of faith. Psalm 119 says that God is a "lamp unto our feet,"[12] not a glaring headlight shining a mile down the road. A lamp for the feet shows one step at a time. You can trust God to lead your next move in life, but don't expect Him to reveal your future.

God is not a fortune teller. He is the Master of all time, and His timing is always perfect. For example, Jesus needed the Apostles to trust His teaching on the Eucharist *before* they could receive Him in the Eucharist. Faith in God leads us one step at a time. If God would have shown me at eighteen years old what I would be doing fifteen years later, I would have never wanted it. I would have walked away from my commitment to Christ, thinking the road of faith too hard and too costly. The trials of faith to come would have seemed excessively demanding. The step of faith God asks us to make today, prepares us for the step of faith tomorrow.

God Is Never Late

Have you ever felt God is taking too long in coming to your aid? This is also a trial of faith. Our impatience with God is an indication of shallow faith. What we are saying to Jesus is that His timing is insufficient, and that our timetable is better.

I am sure Mary and Martha felt this way when their brother Lazarus lay dying. Hoping for a miracle, they sent word for Jesus to come. But when Jesus received the news, He purposely delayed coming to their town for a couple of days.[13] When Mary and Martha prayed, Jesus delayed and their brother Lazarus died. By the time Jesus showed up on the scene, it appeared He was late by four days.

Mary and Martha both said to Jesus, "Lord, if you had been here, my brother would not have died."[14] In their minds, Jesus had let them down, but Jesus knew His timing was perfect. He also knew the pain this delay had caused because of their lack of faith. "When Jesus saw (Mary) weeping, and the Jews who came with her also weeping, he was deeply moved in spirit and troubled."[15]

When we feel Jesus is four days too late, He is not indifferent to our pain. He continues to be greatly troubled when our trouble overwhelms us. But remember that if it seems God is late, a greater glory will be revealed than if He worked by our timetable.

Jesus asked them to remove the stone from the tomb then prayed:

"Father, I thank you for having heard me. I knew that you always hear me, but I have said this for the sake of the crowd standing here, so *that they may believe* that you sent me [emphasis added]." When he had said this, he cried with a loud voice, "Lazarus, come out!" The dead man came out, his hands and feet bound with strips of cloth, and his face wrapped in a cloth. Jesus said to them, "Unbind him, and let him go."[16]

Jesus' delay was allowed so that they would believe. It was a trial of faith. It wasn't that He didn't care that Lazarus had died and the family was mourning. It was because Jesus loved them that their trust was tried. How much more Mary, Martha, Lazarus and the people gained through this trial than if Jesus would have followed their agenda.

If God seems late, it is because you are early. You can trust God's aid to come right when you need it. He will never be late.

Trials of Life Are the Green Houses of Faith

God will never cease purifying your faith in this life. He will continually call you to Himself by the trials He allows. Do not become discouraged and walk away when you do not understand. The trials of life are the green houses of faith. Each ordeal is carefully tended to by our loving Father so that the gift of faith might spring up, bearing much fruit. Each trial is lovingly calculated so that the optimum spiritual growth can be realized.

❦

When you pray and God delays, or the question "why me" goes unanswered, or if life's pressures are suffocating and you are threatened by circumstances, rejoice, for God is loving you. Entrust yourself to Him alone. His hand is pressing upon you so your faith would shine like a diamond.

Chapter Twelve

Mary, Our Perfect Model
Of Surrender

Behold, I am the handmaid of the Lord;
let it be to me according to your word.
~ Mary, the Mother of Jesus ~

Elvis Presley impersonators impersonate the King of Rock and Roll. But as good as they are at shaking their hips, raising their eyebrows, and speaking in a low southern accent, they will never become him.

As Christians, we are not just to act like Jesus, but we are to allow the King of Kings to live through us. It is much more than doing what Jesus would do; it is allowing Him to radically possess every thought, motive, and action. We must be more than impersonators of our Savior. We must become the One whom we receive in the sacraments. As we surrender to the graces of our baptism, the Holy Spirit will consume and transform us into the image of Christ.

The Holy Spirit's possession of you is God's purpose for your life. This does not take away from your identity; rather it forms you into the person you've been created to be. It will happen as we grow in the gift of faith, but sin prevents us from fully realizing this on earth. There is only one who lived this to perfection. That person is Mary, the mother of Jesus. She was fully alive in the Holy Spirit.

Mary Was Hand-Picked

God is the only person in history who has been able to choose His own mother. Now place yourself in God the Father's position for a moment. The selection of your caregiver is a major decision. Tremendous thought would be given in choosing the person who would carry your son in her womb. Wouldn't you want a mom full of compassion and love, worthy of conceiving the perfect gift of your son? Wouldn't you desire a woman who would represent your plan of salvation and cooperate with your saving mission? Wouldn't you want a perfect mother, free from sin, perfect in faith, and a model of holiness? If you were God, the All Holy and Almighty One, it would be unimaginable to settle for a mom less than this.

The truth is, God chose the perfect woman to be His mother. The Church teaches that Mary is the Mother of God, free from sin, and that she is our perfect model of faith. She was conceived without sin, never did sin, remained a virgin her entire life, including during the birth of Jesus, and was assumed into heaven. These beliefs in Mary are not inventions of the Catholic Church, as some would suggest, but have been believed and taught since the beginning of Christianity. To learn more about Marian doctrine and why the Church teaches what it does, visit www.catholic.com.

Bad News Resulted in the Conception of the "Good News"

Imagine being a young woman, engaged. A few weeks before your wedding, an unexpected visitor shows up on your door step. It's an angel. Surprise! You are shocked, but his words shock you even more, "Hail favored one, and because you are so favored you are going to conceive and have a child."

If I were that young woman I think my response would be, "What? Who me?" or "I think you've got the wrong address," or "How am I going to work this out with my fiancé?"

Sounds like an unplanned pregnancy doesn't it? When I think of God's favor, I think of blessing and a life of ease going together. The Kingdom of God doesn't always work that way. Mary was definitely a favored one, but a life of ease was not something God had planned for her. The possibility of pregnancy before marriage would have brought much disgrace to herself, her family and even Joseph.

As Mary pondered the angel's words during the annunciation, maybe Deuteronomy 22:23-24 was running through her mind. It states what should happen to an engaged women who sleeps with another man outside of marriage:

> If there is a betrothed virgin, and a man meets her in the city and lies with her, then you shall bring them both out to the gate of that city, and you shall stone them to death.[1]

The angel's announcement could have been considered a death sentence for Mary. To the eyes of Joseph, and others, it would have appeared that she had slept with another man. The Jewish law was clear. The consequence for this was stoning. Yet Mary submitted her will to God saying, "Behold, I am the handmaid of the Lord; let it be to me according to your word."[2] She was willing to sacrifice herself for the will of the Lord. This is true love.

A love that will not sacrifice for the beloved is no love

at all. Mary loved God above herself, and with her "yes" she entrusted her will to His. It is ironic that the seemingly bad news accepted by Mary resulted in the conception of *Good News* ... Jesus the Messiah. Her faith in God opened the way of salvation for all. St. Irenaeus in the second century said, "The knot of Eve's disobedience was untied by Mary's obedience; what the virgin Eve bound through her disbelief, Mary loosened by her faith."[3]

Where There Is Humility There Is Extravagance

Mary, the mother of the King of Kings, is a perfect model of humility. If there ever were anyone who had the right to brag a bit it was her. Again, imagine an angel appearing to you saying, "Hail, full of grace, the Lord is with you!"[4] Then the heavenly being goes on to say that you will have a son and His kingdom will have no end.[5] Wouldn't you be thinking, "Yeah, I got something right! My son's going to be a king." When good news comes our way, we tend to look at how it will benefit us. Not Mary. She was not distracted by God's promise, but emptied herself before God, humbly calling herself "the handmaid of the Lord."

When the angel left Mary, it seems so did the grand promises of Jesus' kingdom. She gave birth, not in the splendor of a palace, but in the humble setting of a stable. It was likely stinky and uncomfortable. This was the last place you'd expect to give birth to a king. Mary was not even in her home of Nazareth, but in Bethlehem for a census.

Shortly after Jesus' birth, she woke up in the middle of the night and death was in the air.

> The Lord appeared to Joseph in a dream and said, "Rise, take the child and his mother, and flee to Egypt, and remain there till I tell you; for Herod is about to search for the child, to destroy him." And he rose and took the child and his mother by night, and departed to Egypt.[6]

How Mary's heart must have clung to her son as Joseph told her the dream. Imagine. Danger was immediately upon them. Perhaps they heard the soldiers in the streets going door to door and the wailing of mothers as their sons were ripped from their arms and murdered. Panic gripped the night. There was no time to wait until daybreak, no time to pack all their belongings or send word back to family about where they were going. They grabbed the few possessions they could and quietly slipped through the darkness. They left family, friends, and all that was familiar, to go to a foreign land. This is not how you would expect a king to be treated, yet Mary placed her faith in the Lord.

We Cannot Outgive the Infinite Giver

If Jesus asked you to give up family and friends for the sake of His kingdom, would you do it? Some might say, "God would never ask me to do such a thing." Well, He asked Mary and Joseph to do exactly that when they fled into Egypt. And notice again that God didn't give Joseph an address. All the angel said was to flee to Egypt. I'd be wondering exactly to where in Egypt I was to flee. It's a pretty big place, and a more definite location would have been my preference. But God required both Mary and Joseph to walk by faith, and their faith shone in that dark night.

God continues to call all people to walk by faith, and sometimes that requires giving up those we love for His higher love. Three minutes ago I had to say goodbye to somebody very special in my life. It is unlikely that I will see her very often anymore. She is my cousin, one of my best friends and confidant. For four years we worked together on a team, ministering to thousands of young people across central Canada. And now she is gone. Her name is Sr. Christina Holzman. She left to join the Dominican Sisters of Mary Mother of the Eucharist.[7] She is seriously discerning a religious vocation with them. Due to her commitment to the religious community, her many friends, her family, and I will have very limited contact with her.

Christina, through an act of faith, is giving up to God those whom she loves for the sake of His Kingdom. This was the call of Mary, and this is the call for every person. Jesus said, "But seek first his kingdom and his righteousness, and all these things shall be yours as well."[8] When God becomes our one desire, He is allowed to be our provider. We need not worry about what we give up for His sake; God will always give more in return. His Divine will should be your only concern, as all else is a distraction from the purpose of your life. St. Therese of Lisieux said, "Let us go forward in peace, our eyes upon heaven, the only one goal of our labors."[9]

It is impossible to outgive God. Even though our ministry saw tremendous fruit with the presence of Sr. Christina, God will bring a much greater glory for His Kingdom through her, if her calling is to be a religious sister. God's will is not always easy, but it is always worth it. There are no regrets when one gives all for God's will. I am sure Mary, the Queen of Heaven, would agree.

Our Extraordinary God Comes to Us in Ordinary Ways

When things seem ordinary, extraordinary faith is often required. Mary's witness during the growing years of Jesus is an example of this. In these silent years, she must have wondered what would become of her son. She was there for Jesus' first step; she heard the first word come out of His mouth and was there for His first hair cut. Everything about Jesus must have seemed so normal. Mary saw Him grow up into a young man, learning the skills of carpentry alongside Joseph. As the years went by, I would have begun to wonder, "Gabriel, isn't my son supposed to be a king, not a tradesman?" For thirty years Jesus lived an ordinary life, yet Mary's extraordinary faith persevered.

Our faith life most often gets distracted by the ordinary day. We go through our regular routine and don't remember the constant presence of God in our lives. Many complain about the boredom of their work, and while doing so, miss the grace their work could gain if offered in union with Christ.

We are distracted by big bank accounts, fancy cars, and saving up enough money for retirement. The advertising world competes for our attention, while the One who loves us the most barely gets a thought during the day. Some are sucked into the glamorous lies of Hollywood. They fantasize about being "one of them." They waste hours watching T.V. shows, getting the latest celebrity gossip, and trying to keep up with the latest trends. They may never study the lives of holy saints, who are the true role models of moral living, nor the life of Mary, the perfect example.

If you know more about celebrities than Catholic Saints, your priorities need to be re-ordered. The saints are models of holiness. Their lives have meaning and continue to make an eternal impact on the world. We when idolize the celebrities, instead of studying the lives of the saints, we give up the saints' merits in order to be entertained by death. Some may consider this strong language, but it is not. The prevailing gospel of Hollywood is get rich, get famous, and live life for yourself, because that is happiness.

This road does not lead to heaven. If you wish to know how holiness is lived, look to the perfect saint, Mary, the mother of Jesus. In her example you will find the road to heaven.

By seeking the sensational, we can miss grace in the simple. Mary embodied simplicity. Some might argue that because there is little said about Mary in the gospels she is of little importance. This couldn't be further from the truth. The fact that there are few mentions of her, points to her virtuous life. She never demanded attention, although she could have, when Jesus attracted the crowds. She never sought fame or fortune, but walked in complete humility. The Angel Gabriel called her "full of grace." Her cousin Elizabeth declared, "Blessed are you among women."[10] But Mary regarded herself a simple handmaid of the Lord. She never considered God's favor upon her as something she had merited by her own strength, but acknowledged Him as her Savior.

God has given you all you need in your present state of life for you to become a saint. His will for you is holiness. If we fail to achieve this in our time here on earth, it is not because He didn't give us the grace; it is because we missed the grace He offered. The difference between us and many of the saints is that they saw each day as an opportunity to grow in the supernatural life of God. St. Thérèse of Lisieux said, "I prefer the monotony of obscure sacrifice to all ecstasies. To pick up a pin for love can convert a soul."[11]

Each and every moment of our life, God draws us to Himself, disguised in the ordinary. He comes to us in a sunset, a struggle, a flower, a person, and in the simple silence of the day. All that He has created is a communication of His goodness and beauty. Our extraordinary God comes to us in ordinary ways. If you struggle with recognizing Him, ask for the intercession of Mary. She was faced with the seemingly ordinary for thirty years.

Mary Meets Jesus

From conception to the cross, Mary trusted God, but it is during the darkness of Good Friday when her faith seemed to shine the most. We don't know how Mary received word that her son Jesus was condemned to death, but how her heart must have ached in that moment.

Imagine the scene of Jesus carrying the cross. Jesus is hunched over, beaten and bloodied. The crown of thorns presses into His skull, and the weight of the wood is too much for his body to handle. His knees buckle, and he falls with the full weight of the cross landing on him, slamming Him into the ground. Laughter rises from the crowd as the soldiers yell at Him to get up. With all His strength He begins to push Himself up, and then He sees her. Mary. Their eyes meet for but a second, then the soldiers push Jesus onward.

The pain of Mary's heart would have been beyond our understanding. The fruit of her womb was being ripped from her life. Her innocent son, who had done no wrong, was going to be crucified. My mind would have raced back to the promise of the angel Gabriel. "He will be great, and will be called the Son of the Most High."[12] I would have questioned how this could be. Was I lied to by God's messenger? But Mary continued to trust in God.

Mary now stands on Calvary. Jesus' life is fading. The soldiers beside her are casting lots for his tunic, and the rulers are mocking Him. Again I would have wondered at the words of the angel. "He will reign over the house of Jacob for ever; and of his kingdom there will be no end."[13] These words must have seemed so far from the truth now. It would appear to be the end, for how can a dead son establish a kingdom? I would have thought, "Did I hear the angel right? It was more than thirty years ago, and now Jesus is dying. I must have misunderstood ... or God has broken His promise." Yet Mary believed in God even when it seemed foolish to believe anymore.

When you are in the face of the cross and it seems that God has abandoned you, remember Mary is beside you, just as she stood by Jesus and heard Him say, "My God, my God, why have you forsaken me?"[14] She stands by you when you feel deserted. When it seems that it is foolish to believe in the goodness of God, remember Mary fully understands. She is our mother of sorrows and is familiar with suffering. She will help you carry the cross through her intercession.

Her "yes" to the will of God, opened the way of salvation for you. From conception to the cross, Mary stood by her son, humbly submitting to the will of God, never questioning her suffering. Mary gave up her son for you. She is the mother of your salvation and wants nothing more than for you to embrace her son Jesus.

> By pronouncing her "fiat" at the Annunciation and giving her consent to the Incarnation, Mary was already collaborating with the whole work her Son was to accomplish.[15]

To Fully Accept Jesus Means to Accept His Mom, Too

When we accept Jesus as our Lord, being faithful to our baptism, we are accepting all that He is. This is the call of every baptized Christian. But to fully accept all that Jesus is means also to accept His mother. You cannot separate the life of Jesus from the life of Mary. We shouldn't say, "I want You Jesus, but I don't want Your mom." Somehow that doesn't seem to honor Christ. It was Mary's "yes" that brought Jesus into the world. It was she who nurtured Him, and it was she who followed Him to the cross. If you wish to fully receive all that Jesus has for you, this means to personally accept Mary as your spiritual mother.

Some mistakenly believe that Catholics worship Mary. This is not so. We give her the honor she deserves, but we do not worship her as a goddess. If you do not acknowledge Mary as the Blessed Virgin and "full of grace,"[16] you are not being faithful to God's word, found in the first chapter of Luke. Also, to honor her is only being Christ-like. Jesus perfectly lived all of God's commands, including "honor your father and your mother."[17] If we are to be Christ-like then we, too, must honor Mary. This is the duty of every Christian. To speak ill of her is wrong and not the way of Jesus.

Wherever Jesus is savior, Mary is mother.[18] Jesus gave His whole life for the world on the cross, and it was fitting that on the cross He gave the world His Mother.

> When Jesus saw his mother, and the disciple whom he loved standing near, he said to his mother, "Woman, behold, your son!" Then he said to the disciple, "Behold, your mother!" And from that hour the disciple took her to his own home.[19]

It is at this point Jesus' mother became our mother, too. The apostle, John, took Mary into his home, accepting her as His own. Mary, being obedient to her Son's word, accepted John as her son and every person in the world as her own child. Being the mother of the redeemer, she became the mother of all who needed redemption. "Mary had only one Son, Jesus, but in him her spiritual motherhood extends to all whom he came to save."[20] We should follow the example of John who embraced Mary as his own, so that Mary will lead us to her son Jesus.

༄

Mary was hand-picked for you. She loves you as she loved her own child, Jesus. She would desire nothing less for you than the will of the Father. You can be sure that asking for Mary's intercession will lead you in God's purpose for your life. The Divine will is the only thing that concerns Mary. She lived for God's purpose, gave her Son for God's purpose, and prays now for God's purpose. Her whole earthly life was lived for the will of God, and her heavenly life continues to be so.

> We believe that the Holy Mother of God, the new Eve, Mother of the Church, continues in heaven to exercise her maternal role on behalf of the members of Christ.[21]

If you desire to experience the fullness of purpose God has for your life, ask Mary to pray for you. Your mom won't let you down.

Chapter Thirteen

The Hinge Of Humility

Do nothing from selfishness or conceit,
but in humility count others better than yourselves.
Philippians 2:3

No man can attain to the knowledge
of God but by humility.
The way to mount high is to descend.
Blessed Giles of Assisi

On the night of August 31, 1986, a tragedy occurred in the Black Sea, a couple of miles off the coast of Russia. Two Soviet vessels, a passenger ship and a cargo liner, collided and sank, drowning 448 people in the freezing water. Upon investigation, the cause of the accident only darkened the tragedy. There hadn't been a radar malfunction or a mechanical failure. The explanation was simple: human pride. Both captains were aware of the pending collision course and refused to slow their ships. While one captain went down to sleep, the other did nothing to change his course. Both refused to give way to the other. By the time they realized disaster was upon them, it was too late. The ships collided, bringing death to many of their innocent passengers. Both captains were sentenced to 15 years in jail for being in violation of navigational safety rules and for criminal negligence.

The sin of pride sank humanity into spiritual death. When God created Adam, He said:

> You may freely eat of every tree of the garden; but of the tree of the knowledge of good and evil you shall not eat, for in the day that you eat of it you shall die.[1]

This command was not to restrict Adam but to keep him free. His obedience to God brought him life, and his disobedience would lead to death.

> But the serpent said to the woman, "You will not die; for God knows that when you eat of it your eyes will be opened, and *you will be like God,* knowing good and evil [emphasis added]."[2]

Wanting to be like God, and not satisfied with being His children, Adam and Eve rejected God's plan and chose the fruit of the tree in hopes of being wise. They believed in their own wisdom, rather than trusting the infinite wisdom of God. The first sin committed was that of pride, and it resulted in loss of friendship with God.

Humility Is the Acknowledgement of Truth

Pride is undue love for self and a rejection of God. It sinks our spiritual ship on our faith's journey and prevents us from growing in God's Divine life. Pride always questions God's truth by echoing the serpent's words in the garden, "Did God say?"[3] Found in the middle of pride is the deception that "my way is better than God's way, because He is withholding goodness from me."

Pride trusts in itself and rejects God's grace. This is a big problem because all that we need to grow in the spiritual life comes from God through grace. "God opposes the proud, but gives grace to the humble."[4] If you want to embrace God's purpose for your life, you have to grow in the gift of humility. This virtue is the doorway that leads to the life of God.

Humility is the acknowledgement of truth. A humble soul sees who he is and admits dependency upon God for everything. This is the door Jesus looks for. He will not impose Himself on the self-sufficient, for then this would not be love. Rather, Jesus exposes our weaknesses so that we will call out in desperation for Him. One who sees their weaknesses, but does not call out to God, cannot be helped. Love always seeks an invitation. It is from a humble heart that an authentic prayer for Jesus arises. Without a cry of humility, we will remain lost in ourselves.

The grace of humility demands that we have a childlike faith. Jesus said:

> Let the children come to me ... for to such belongs the kingdom of God.... Whoever does not receive the kingdom of God like a child shall not enter it.[5]

Children quickly ask for help when they begin to fail. How often we forget to do this because we are busy trying to come up with our own solution. St. Paul said, "Whenever I am weak, then I am strong."[6] Acknowledging our helplessness allows our Divine Helper to assist us. As long as we believe we are fine on our own, we remain out of reach from the hand of God.

A childlike faith quickly admits its need. When a toddler falls down hard and bangs his or her knee, you quickly know the child is hurt. A high-pitched scream pierces the air, and all the dogs in the neighborhood start barking. The youngster does not pretend to be okay, but rather goes running to mom or dad. He or she knows that an embrace by loving arms is the perfect Band-Aid for a skinned knee. This is the kind of faith we need to have in our heavenly Father. To welcome the healing touch of God, we must humble ourselves and recognize our pain. We must not stuff our hurt down inside, pretending it isn't there.

There Is Freedom in Humility

Any habitual sin or negative pattern of thought in your life is often rooted in the pain of the past. We must allow God to show us the cause of why we act out and think as we do. We must humbly beg Him to speak to us in the pain of previous events, because His words will bring healing. Jesus came to set the captives free. It is a humbling thing to say that we are hurt, but acknowledging the truth is what humility does, and when truth is proclaimed, freedom can grow. Jesus said, "The truth will make you free."[7]

Jesus is the perfect model of humility. He gave up the company of angels and the glory of heaven to be confined to a human body. Imagine how humbling it would be if you became an ant for thirty-three years. How much more so for Jesus, Second Person of the Trinity, to become flesh in a finite body. In heaven, every angel stood at attention waiting for

His command, yet Jesus, who was fully God and fully man, became obedient to Mary and Joseph. Wisdom Himself now grew up under the wisdom of man. The Master of time was subject to sleep. The Creator of food needed to eat. Jesus is the definition of humility. "He humbled himself and became obedient to the point of death – even death on a cross."[8]

The Eucharist Is the Humility of God Before Our Eyes

Humility demands we not trust in mere appearance. The Eucharist is the humility of God before our eyes. Jesus disguises Himself under the appearance of bread and wine, yet He is fully alive and totally present in the consecrated gifts. Like all mysteries of our faith, what appears not to be, is. The Eucharist is Jesus' flesh and blood, yet it does not appear so. In awesome humility, Christ places Himself defenseless in our hands during the mass. His body is at our mercy! Through the Eucharist, Jesus gives us a glimpse of what loving humility looks like. Humility is offering oneself in love to be consumed.

The Eucharistic Jesus does not demand, but simply gives to us. We must place ourselves before God in this humble fashion. We must allow Him to consume and do with us whatever He wills. We must be willing to expose all that we are before Him and be broken if need be. Just as Jesus is placed into our hands at mass, we must lovingly give ourselves to Him without reserve.

The humility of Jesus in the Eucharist also teaches us how we must love others. I recently saw a documentary about Mother Teresa of Calcutta. She encouraged her sisters by saying, "Let the people eat you up."[9] She was asking her members to offer the same love to the people as Jesus offered them in the Eucharist every morning. Just as they consumed Jesus through the Eucharist, they were to allow themselves to be consumed by the people they served. Jesus set the example of love by giving us the Eucharist saying, "Take, eat; this is my body."[10] The sisters were to love with the same Eucharistic heart. They were to serve the poorest of the poor by offering themselves entirely.

We must not mistakenly think that this type of love is only for the religious, but for all. Jesus said, "I give you a new commandment ... just as I have loved you, you also should love one another."[11] How did Jesus love? He said, "Take, this is my body." When we receive the Eucharist, we should do so with the desire to become Eucharist for those around us. At the end of mass the priest says, "Go to love and serve the Lord." We must give ourselves to the service of the world in union with Christ. This does not necessarily demand that we change our state of life, but it does mean a change of heart.

Instead of living for ourselves during the day, let us choose to offer all as a sacrifice: joys and sorrows, our seen and unseen work, all offered for the purpose of God, in union with Jesus. A humble heart does not demand to be served, but looks for opportunities to offer interior sacrifice for others. Jesus said:

> Whoever wishes to be first among you must be your slave; just as the Son of Man came not to be served but to serve, and to give his life as a ransom for many.[12]

We must die to ourselves in order to love others.

Humility Washes the Feet of Others

A prideful heart is focused on the failures of others and thinks of itself as superior. This was not the way of Jesus, although He had the right to act this way. During the Last Supper, He offered us an example of humility. Jesus took off His outer robe, tied a towel around Himself, and knelt down to wash the feet of His Apostles. Twelve men in that room would have been asked to remove their sandals after walking all day. I can only image the stench. I know what my feet smell like after hiking for a day, and I can tell you they ain't smellin' like roses. That room must have reeked with body odor and sweaty feet, and Jesus went to the source of the stench.

Imagine Jesus kneeling before His Apostles, washing their feet and remembering the last three years. He is before Peter thinking: "I love these feet. I have called them from the sea to be a fisher of my people. These feet were there when the sick were healed, the lame walked, and the deaf heard. These feet stood on the mountain of transfiguration and saw my glory. These feet have even walked on water. These feet will eventually lead others to me, but soon they will abandon me at Calvary and run away, *clean.* I love these feet."

Jesus kneels down before Judas Iscariot, perhaps thinking the following: "I love these feet. For three years these feet have walked with me, and they have seen and heard so much. These feet went through the crowds, feeding five thousand people with five loaves of bread and two fish; these feet were at Jericho and saw the two blind men healed; they were there when Peter proclaimed, 'You are the Christ, the Son of the living God.'[13] And in a few moments these feet will run from this room, *clean,* and deny me for thirty pieces of silver. How I love these feet."

Jesus, the King of all kings was kneeling before men the night of the Last Supper. Instead of a royal robe over His shoulders, He tied a rag around His waist. He washed clean the feet that ran from Him. That is humility: to serve those who would abandon you; to help others, knowing they will not help you; and to treat those with dignity who act undignified towards you.

After washing their feet, Jesus said, "For I have set you an example, that you also should do as I have done to you."[14] His humble act of love is to be imitated by us. Who are the Peters in your life? They are those close to you who have not followed you to Calvary. When you were in need, they did not stand by your side. Will you wash their feet? Would you help them if they had not helped you? Who are the Judases in your life? They are those who have rejected your friendship and abused your trust. If they would need your aid, would you give it? Humility does not focus on others' failures; instead, it washes the feet of those who have run from us.

Humility Sees All as Grace

A humble person recognizes he is capable of committing every evil in the world, but acknowledges it is only God's grace protecting him from this. Take, for example, the sin of murder. A person with a prideful heart harshly judges those who have sinned this way. He thinks, "Oh, I could never do that," believing himself to be beyond such an evil act. The truth is that God's grace, and not our "goodness," leads us not to sin this way. Therefore, a humble person is nonjudgmental and forgiving, because he recognizes others' sin as his own, if not for the grace of God. This is the truth. In humility this person is aware of his own spiritual need.

As God's light shines upon the hearts of individuals, revealing their capacity for evil, the grace of humility allows those individuals to accept this and realize all the more deeply that they are the beloved of the Father.

Your life is a gift from God. You did not ask to be born nor have you done anything to merit yourself deserving of life. God in His kindness brought you into existence to share with you Himself and to give to you eternal happiness. He did not have to create you, but chose to do so; therefore, everything in your life is a gift from God. All is grace.

Persons realizing God's graciousness toward them, fall deeper in love with Him with each degree of this understanding. Those struggling with pride perceive their life as their own. When things don't go their way, they focus on exercising their rights for selfish reasons. A humble person knows his life belongs to God and is willing to yield his right to be right.

When faced with criticism, how do you react? A prideful response is to be defensive when criticized. A humble reaction would be to receive criticism with openness. There are two reasons why you never have to be defensive again. The first is because the person criticizing you is *wrong*. Listen with humility; you do not have to rigorously justify yourself, because faithfulness to God is your only concern. Your identity is not in the words of another, but in the truth that you are a child of God. The second reason you never have to be defensive when criticized is because the person criticizing you is *right*. And if the criticizer is right, then you should listen and change. A humble response, again, is only concerned with faithfulness to God and is quick to admit fault. Now you need never be defensive in your life again.

How you participate in the sacrament of reconciliation is a good indication of where your heart is. When confessing sin, are you specific or general? A person struggling with pride might confess in generalities. He is worried about his image and hides behind the vagueness of his admission. Sometimes, in pride, a person doesn't want to confess face-to-face with a priest, but instead hides behind the screen of a confessional. The worry is over his reputation rather than the seriousness of his sin. As such, he robs himself of an opportunity to grow in the grace of humility, by humbling himself before the eyes of another. A humble person is grieved over his sin and believes all that matters is what God knows. His concern is reconciliation and not reputation.

How much time do you spend worrying about your religious exterior, rather than the interior motivation of your heart? The *appearance* of our goodness matters nothing in the Kingdom of God. "Beware of practicing your piety before others in order to be seen by them; for then you have no reward from your Father in heaven."[15] When you serve your community or church, do you anticipate being acknowledged for your service? If so, you serve your religious reputation rather than Christ. It is a privilege to serve others, because by reaching to them we serve Jesus. This should be reward enough! It is the service of Him that is our joy, not the praise of others.

Bribery is bestowing a gift to influence the recipient's conduct. Consider this in a spiritual sense. So often our charitable works are done with selfish motivation. We may even render a good deed so as to give ourselves the right to recall the favor in the future, or at the very least be esteemed by those whom we have helped. This is not love, but spiritual bribery! Serving others in love should not leave you thinking, "They owe me."

This spiritual bribery can be as simple as expecting or demanding to be thanked. Love does not count the cost. It is our Christian duty to serve others, not an option. We don't serve a "thank-you," we serve Christ. If a thank-you comes your way, rejoice; and if it does not, rejoice anyway. Our God is faithful and perfectly just. You cannot outgive the Infinite Giver.

So do not worry about your reward and thanks. Our heavenly Father will take care of that. John 12:26 says, "Whoever serves [Jesus], the Father will honor."[16] If we worry about our "thank-you," it is as though we say to our heavenly Father, "Your honor is not enough." Isn't the honor you will receive from Him sufficient for you? If we serve with love, our heavenly Father will far surpass any temporary affirmation by others with an eternal weight of glory.

The Door of Love Swings on the Hinge of Humility

Revelations 3:20 says, "Behold, I stand at the door and knock; if any one hears my voice and opens the door, I will come in to him and eat with him, and he with me."[17]

Humility is the hinge on which the door of love swings. It is by this grace that Jesus is able to enter our lives. Without it, there will be no heaven for us. God will be sure to provide many opportunities for us to grow in this grace. It is through humiliations that we grow in humility. You can read all about this grace, but it is when you are defeated that it can truly grow in your life.

Consider all your failures and broken dreams as God's invitation to grow in humility. It is through these experiences that you will realize your nothingness without Him. It is in these places of brokenness that Jesus knocks on the door of your heart. Therefore, rejoice in times of humiliation; it is in these moments that God is oiling the rusty hinge of humility on which the door of love swings.

Chapter Fourteen

The Encounter Of God's Thirst
With Ours

*Don't imagine that, if you had a great deal of time, you
would spend more of it in prayer. Get rid of that idea; it is
no hindrance to prayer to spend your time well.*
St. Teresa of Avila

One early fall morning an elderly father and his strong,
youthful son headed out into the woods to cut down trees for
firewood. As they walked, with their axes in their hands, the
son asked his father, "If I cut down more trees than you, may I
take the extra wood and sell it at the town market?"

The father replied, "Every tree you cut beyond the
number of mine, you may do with it whatever you like."

The son was eager, knowing his endurance and strength
surpassed his father's. He was sure to cut many more trees and
make a handsome profit for his day's work.

From the very beginning, it was clear the father was
no match for his son's power and stamina. The son worked
consistently all day, not even stopping for breaks. When the
father was tired, he sat and rested; but the son pushed on,
powerfully swinging his axe, determined to make a big profit.
At the end of the day, the father and son began to count the
trees each had cut. To the son's surprise, the father had cut
down twice as many trees.

Exasperated, the son asked, "How is it that I worked harder and longer, even skipping breaks, yet you cut twice the number of trees that I did?"

The father replied, "While you worked during the breaks, I was sharpening my axe."

Prayer Is the Plan of God

Without prayer, we would be swinging away at life, missing the intentions of God. Let us go back to the basics. Do you remember what the purpose of your life is? To know, love, and serve God, and share His eternal glory forever in heaven.

Let us examine again what it is to know God. How can we know somebody unless we spend time with him? Wouldn't it seem silly to claim that I know the Queen of England, although I have never met her, or spent time in her presence? You would call me a liar or delusional! Likewise, how can we claim to know Jesus, the King of Kings, unless we spend time in His presence?

Brother Lawrence said prayer is practicing the presence of God. You can know all you want about God, memorize theologies and dogmas, but unless you pray, it will profit your soul nothing. St. Alphonsus Liguori put it more simply, "Those who pray are certainly saved. Those who do not pray are certainly damned."[1] The point is this, do you pray? Because if not, you will miss the purpose of your life!

You are designed to know God, which is Jesus' definition of eternal life. "Now this is eternal life: that they may know you, the only true God, and Jesus Christ, whom you have sent."[2] It is by spending time with Jesus that we will come to know Him; therefore, pray! It is God's plan for your life, and your eternal resting place is at stake.

What is more important to you, your soul or your body? Imagine, somebody offers you the choice between a great conditioned body and a soul in terrible condition, *or* a homely looking body and a great conditioned soul. Think twice before choosing! Keep in mind that your body will not last forever, but your soul will. Your body will return to the dust of the earth, but your soul cannot be destroyed. Your body, if in great condition now, will eventually wear out and get old. On the other hand, the soul does not wear out. It will remain forever in one of two places, heaven or hell. It is eternal.

It is the soul that makes you, you. A great conditioned body is not your identity. What if you were to lose your arm, would you still be you? Yes. How about lose a leg and an ear? Would you still be you? Yes. You get old, wrinkly, and put on fifty pounds, would you still be you? Yes. What makes you, *you,* is your soul.

Now then, back to the question, which one do you choose: a great conditioned body or a great conditioned soul? I assume you will say the soul. My question then would be, is this reflected in how you spend your time?

Are you more dedicated to your dieting than to your prayer time? During the day, do you commit more mental discipline to counting the number of calories you consume than to thinking about Jesus? Do you spend more effort exercising your body through workouts, than exercising your soul through prayer? Do you arise early in the morning to get to the gym, but neglect to spend time with the Lord of the morning? Is the gym your Lord? There is nothing wrong with exercise, but when it becomes a higher priority than prayer, we have an imbalance.

It is quite simple; if your soul is a priority, then consistent daily prayer will be also. After all, if you can find time to exercise daily, then you can find time to pray daily. They are both great disciplines, but only one has an eternal significance.

The impossible is made possible through prayer. One of the greatest miracles that can happen is when a sinner is transformed into a saint. By our own strength, this is unattainable. Sainthood cannot occur through natural means. We need supernatural help. Prayer moves us deeper into the supernatural life of God, allowing Him to do what we cannot: make us holy. Thus the impossible is made possible. St. John Chrysostom said:

> Nothing is equal to prayer, for what is impossible it makes possible, what is difficult easy.... For it is impossible, utterly impossible for the man who prays eagerly and invokes God ceaselessly ever to sin.[3]

If you want to be holy, then you have to pray.

Prayer is air for your soul. No prayer, no life. You know what happens when you stop breathing. Try it successfully, and you won't finish this chapter. Eventually your body dies. What happens when you stop praying? The life of God is suffocated in your soul. God's life within us builds upon our response to Him. When we stop responding to God, we cut off the One who gives us life. Our faith and faithfulness to Him will suffer if prayer is neglected.

If we stop praying, our faith will die. If our faith dies, so then will our service, for our service is faith in action. Removing prayer from the Christian life causes everything to fall apart. Our trust in God will diminish, and if we do not trust Him, we will not obey and love Him.

I've often heard people say they wish they had more faith. My response is, pray more! Faith will not magically grow in your life. You must nurture the seed of faith with prayer. It will increase your faith. Likewise, I've often heard people wishing they had more strength to be faithful to God. Again, pray more! Disobedience and a lack of faith within the Church are common fruits of prayerlessness. The more you pray, the more your faith will grow. The more you pray, the more your faithfulness will grow. Remember, it is impossible for you, if you pray constantly, ever to be unfaithful.

Jesus should be our first love; therefore, He deserves our quality time. Pick a time and place during the day, where you are free from distractions, for personal prayer. Your prayer time is an encounter with the One who loves you the most. Anticipate and look forward to this time in the day. Jesus is excited to have your attention.

Your life is constantly before Him. Even your words are known by Him before you say them, and with each passing moment He thinks, "There is my beloved with whom I am well pleased." How Jesus must eagerly wait for the time we give Him during the day for prayer. For here He finally has our attention. What joy it must bring to His heart!

If you have never established a prayer time, think about how long Jesus has been waiting. He does not wait with impatience, rather with great anticipation for you. Your words are a symphony of consolation to Him, even if they are not said with perfect devotion. It is not the words He wants, but the heart behind the words.

According to St. Augustine, "Whether we realize it or not, prayer is the encounter of God's thirst with ours. God thirsts that we may thirst for him."[4] How it must delight His heart when we are quiet before Him in prayer, surrendering our whole self to Him. Finally, for but a brief second, He has our undivided attention.

Isn't it ironic that the One who constantly gives us His undivided attention waits for ours? He sees us running around in our day, forgetting Him and even purposely ignoring Him, yet He waits for that precise moment of silence when all we contemplate is Him. To sit in silence with the one He loves, to lovingly stare into the eyes of His beloved and whisper words of life to the heart, this is what He has been waiting for. He waits to give Himself to you.

Much of my time from September to June is spent on the road speaking and leading worship. For the past five years, at the end of our ministry year in June, I have gone on a fishing trip in the Canadian Shield to rejuvenate. Anchoring the boat in a small secluded bay on a calm summer evening is an experience to which I look forward every trip.

The stillness of the water is breathtaking, acting like a mirror, reflecting everything around it. As I stare out onto the lake I can see the beauty of the trees, the rocks, and the setting of the sun all reflected in the water before me. These moments are precious because they don't happen every day. Only when the waters are still, can they reflect the beauty of creation surrounding them. When the wind comes, so do the waves, and the reflection is gone.

I often think of this image when reflecting on the words in Palms 46, "Be still and know that I am God."[5] Only when we quiet ourselves before the Lord can we begin to reflect His image. In silence we can come to know Him as our God. The noisiness of life creates waves in our souls. We must quiet ourselves before God in humble submission. In silence we should allow Jesus to possess us, giving up all our rights.

A Noisy Life Tends to Lead to Self-Centeredness

Our society tends to be afraid of stillness. Think about the last time you experienced the so-called "awkward silence" in a social gathering. A three-second lull in the conversation, and we want to crawl underneath a rock and die. We have been conditioned to be comfortable in noise. Walk into a mall and you will find every store has music playing in the background; when put on hold, you get the company jingle; step into a car and the first thing you do is put on the radio or your favorite CD. Even homes are places of noise. The T.V is constantly on; music is coming from a bedroom; the phone is ringing. Jesus has to compete very hard for your attention! He just wants to be with you, so please give Him that opportunity.

When we fill our lives with noise, life tends to be about us. We speak of our favorite song, our favorite artist, our favorite T.V show. A noisy life gradually leads to a very self-centered life. Even our prayer can be very noisy, and the noisier our prayer time is, the more self-centered it can become. We tell God what we want. We instruct Him on what to do. We complain when things do not go our way. Having silence in our prayer creates an environment where we take our eyes off of ourself, and place them on God. Remember, life is not about us, it is about Him. So prayer is the only right response to the circumstances we find ourselves in. Silence helps create that right response.

Do you have silence in your prayer time? A simple exercise I often do to still myself before Jesus is simply to take deep breaths. As I breathe in I think, "Jesus consume me." As I breathe out I think, "Take all of me." In this way our breath can become a prayer. If you can breathe, you can pray! This helps me quiet my heart and mind. Eventually, if the grace of God allows, let these phrases slip away, and be before God in this receptive manner. If distracting thoughts arise, resume the simple phrases mentioned or allow the Holy Spirit to form your own.

Prayer Increases Our Faith

We should approach prayer like a little child comes to his father. A child's words are simple and direct. Children do not speak in complicated language but say what they mean and share how they feel. Let your prayer be simple like that. Say what you mean. Acknowledge how you feel. You do not need to impress God with fancy religious language. He is already impressed with you because you are His child, made in His image and likeness. He wants your heart, not poetic language. So give Him what He is thirsty for: your whole life.

Some do not like to pray because they feel they are not good at it, like someone who has been asked to sing a song, but is afraid to do it for fear of being off pitch. Prayer is not something you can fail at. You are always on perfect pitch when you turn your heart to God, because you are being who you have been created to be. You are designed to be in communion with Him. You mess prayer up simply by not praying!

Another hesitation in prayer can be the feeling that you are not accomplishing anything. Consider this, do two people who are in love hold each other in their arms and think, "This is a waste of time, I am not accomplishing anything." Prayer is not about accomplishing a goal but about being with somebody you love. When a man and a woman are in love, they are not focused on counting down the number of minutes they are with each other. Each moment is cherished. It is not what they do together that matters, but the fact that they are together. Prayer can be considered like this. It is never a wasted moment, when you spend it with God. He is the One who has created the moment, and you never know if you will have another chance to respond to Him.

The eloquence of your words does not matter to Him. It is you who He wants and not your words. Be convinced that simply saying the name of Jesus with love and humility just once is worth more than saying it a thousand times without devotion to Him. St. John Chrysostom said, "Whether or not our prayer is heard depends not on the number of words, but on the fervour of our souls."[6] Prayer is not a goal to be accomplished, but an intimate encounter with God.

Jesus taught His Apostles to pray the words, "Thy will be done." In every intention laid before God, we must not try to impose our will upon His. For example, praying for the success of our daily activities, such as school, work, or finances, may not be God's will. He may desire that these activities fail. This may seem as a shock to some. Why would God desire failure? The answer is that this might be the best thing for our souls. If we love His blessing more than we love Him, then our love is misplaced. If what we are praying for is getting in the way of our love for Him, or if He desires us to grow in the grace of humility, then failure may be the loving thing to allow. A single person who is asking God to "send me that special someone" may miss God's call to the single or religious vocation. Our wants are not necessarily God's will.

We should not presume to know the will of God in every circumstance. When making a request before God, we should always be mindful to say, "not my will but Yours be done." Ultimately, His will, and His alone, is what will satisfy our hearts. Don't settle for less. You deserve the best. The best is His will, so pray like Jesus said to pray: "Thy will be done."

Prayer Impacts Eternity

I was once praying about the words from the Our Father, "Thy will be done." I was considering what they meant to me when a simple thought came into my mind. Could it be that if I do not pray, "Thy will be done," His will might not happen? Through prayer, God invites us to accomplish His will on earth. Prayer can change history, soften hearts, avert natural disasters, bring down governments opposed to "His will," and impact eternity! It is a privilege to pray. We have the immediate attention of God Almighty when we say, "Father, Your will be done." Let the following story be an encouragement to you regarding intercessory prayer.

A few years ago, my team and I were leading a youth and family retreat in northern Saskatchewan in a small, rural town in the middle of winter. We ended Saturday evening in an anointed time of musical Eucharistic adoration, where we had witnessed many first-time commitments to Christ and renewals of faith.

At about half-past midnight, the four of us left the church with our ministry van to travel to a farmhouse for the night. We had been given directions to the yard, but it was very difficult to tell where we were going on the country roads; there were no signs and a think layer of fog was hanging in the night air, making the visibility very limited. We were all very tired after a day of ministry, and the time was nearing one a.m. We all wanted to get to bed as soon as possible because we had a full day coming up.

After some time of driving, we realized I had taken a wrong turn and needed to backtrack to the highway off of which we had turned. Very impatient and frustrated, I turned around and sped up, in hopes to make up for lost time. My plan was to go fast for the first bit through the fog, then slow down after a couple of fields before the 'T' intersection. Unfortunately, I miscalculated the number of fields and suddenly, emerging from the thick fog, was the stop sign.

I slammed on the brakes, which did nothing on the icy road, then immediately had two thoughts: one, we could slide through the intersection, hoping no cars would sideswipe us, and take our chances with the ditch straight ahead; or two, try to turn, and hope we don't flip. For some reason I chose two. I cranked the wheel, and the van made a ninety-degree turn without any effort at all. We found ourselves safely on the highway, in complete silence. Then one of the team members said, "We were just preserved." We all knew it. There was no way our van could have made that turn at the speed we had been going, especially considering the icy road conditions.

A day after this retreat, one of my team members went to visit her sister. Immediately upon opening the door of the house, her sister said, "I had a terrible dream about you and the team Saturday night. I dreamt you were traveling and got into a car accident. In the dream, Ken was killed. It was so startling that it woke me up, and I said a quick prayer for the group then went back to sleep."

My team member asked her sister what time she had woken up. She replied, "Around one a.m." ... approximately the same time as our near accident.

We will never know what would have happened that evening if no prayer had been sent our way, but we all had a sense we had been protected by the hand of God. Prayer makes a difference!

 co&

God has a wonderful plan in store for you, but He will not impose it upon your life. It will only be discovered through a life of prayer. Just as our eyes need light to see, we need prayer to grow in knowledge and love of God. As you respond to the thirst of God by seeking Him in prayer, your life will take on God's intentions.

Living according to the teachings of the Catholic Church is the surest road to reaching our full God-given potential. Within Christ's Church the fullness of truth subsists, leading each person to greatness.

Imagine a baby eagle being raised by a mother hen in a chicken coup; the eaglet may never learn to soar to great heights. It may miss its purpose because it will never learn the full truth about its identity. Soaring high in the sky may not be an option for an eagle, if it thinks it is a chicken.

Likewise we may never soar to our full potential if not led by the fullness of truth. God desires us to spread our wings and open our hearts to rise to great intimacy with Him. The truth will lead us there. It is the truth that sets us free.

Let us embrace the fullness of truth, to live out the fullness of our purpose. Then, by His grace, may we each become who God created us to be ... a great saint!

End Notes

Excerpts from *Catechism of the Catholic Church,*
Copyright © Concacan Inc., 1999
All rights reserved.

Excerpts from *Compendium of the Catechism of the Catholic Church,*
Copyright © Concacan Inc., 2006
All rights reserved.

Chapter 1 – Full Purpose, Full Potential

1 Matthew 16:18
2 1 Corinthians 2:9, NRSV

Chapter 2 – Created to Know God

1 Catechism of the Catholic Church, par 1
2 Catechism of the Catholic Church, par 1
3 John 10:14
4 Pope John Paul II, speech to bishops of Southern Germany, Dec. 4, 1992. L'Osservatore Romano (English ed.), Dec. 23/30, 1992, pp. 5-6.
5 Act 26:5
6 Philippians 3:8, NRSV
7 Pope John Paul II, L'Osservatore Romano (English Edition of the Vatican Newspaper), March 24, 1993, p.3).
8 Gal 2:20, NRSV
9 Genesis 1:3-4
10 Genesis 1:31
11 Compendium of the Catechism of the Catholic Church, section 1
12 Catechism of the Catholic Church, par 30
13 1 John 4:8
14 Spitz, R. A. In, The Psychoanalytic Study of the Child, Vols. 1-4, New York: International Universities Press, 1945-49
15 Spitz, R. A. Hospitalism: A follow-up report. In, D. Fenichel, P. Greenacre & A. Freud (Eds.), The Psychoanalytic Study of the Child, Vol. 2, New York: International Universities Press, 1947, 113-117
16 John Paul II, Encyclical Letter, Redemptor hominis, March 4, 1979, section 10
17 St. Thomas Aquinas, Expositio in symbolum. apostolicum. I.
18 Luke 16:13, RSVCE
19 Revelations 3:20, RSVCE

Chapter 3 – You Are Passionately Loved

1 http://www.auschwitz.dk/Kolbe.htm
2 http://www.jewishvirtuallibrary.org/jsource/

biography/Kolbe.html
3 http://www.auschwitz.dk/Kolbe.htm
4 Catechism of the Catholic Church, par 616
5 Matthew 26:37
6 Luke 22:42, NRSV
7 Luke 22:44
8 Lumpkin, R. (1978), "The Physical Suffering of Christ," Journal of Medical Association of Alabama, 47:8-10.
9 "Compendium of the Catechism of the Catholic Church," paragraph 121
10 Luke 22:46
11 Matthew 26:50, NRSV
12 John 18:10
13 Matthew 26:53, RSVCE
14 Catechism of the Catholic Church, par 600
15 Catechism of the Catholic Church, par. 598
16 John 19:1, RSVCE
17 Bucklin, R, (1970), " The Legal and Medical Aspects of the Trial and Death of Christ," Reprinted from Medicine, Science and the Law, January, 1970
18 Isaiah 53:5, RSVCE
19 Matthew 27:32
20 Mark 15:31, RSVCE
21 John 11:43, RSVCE
22 John 11:44, RSVCE
23 1 Corinthians 15:3, RSVCE
24 Catechism of the Catholic Church, par. 615
25 Luke 23:34, RSVCE
26 John 19:28, RSVCE
27 John 19:30, RSVCE

Chapter 4 – Becoming The Beloved

1 Mathew 28:19, RSVCE
2 Matthew 19:6, RSVCE
3 Catechism of the Catholic Church, par 796
4 Catechism of the Catholic Church, par 418-419
5 Catechism of the Catholic Church , par 518
6 Catechism of the Catholic Church, par 605
7 Philippians 2:10-11, RSVCE
8 Mathew 29:19, RSVCE
9 Mark 1:11, NRSV

10 John 10:30, RSVCE
11 John 8:28, NRSV
12 Ephesians 1:11-12
13 Psalm 71:6
14 Hebrew 12:1
15 1 Corinthians 3:16
16 Compendium of the Catechism of the Catholic Church, par 63
17 Compendium of the Catechism of the Catholic Church, par 1265
18 Catechism of the Catholic Church, par 1253
19 Second Vatican Council, *"Constitution on Divine Revelation,"* no.5
20 Change reference to: *"A Personal Pentacost"*, from the Goodnews archives, May/June 2010. http://www.ccr.org.uk/archive/gn1005/g02.htm
21 Pope John Paul II, *Encyclical Letter Mission of the Redeemer* (1990) 46.

Chapter 5 – Made For Freedom

1 Genesis 2:17, RSVCE
2 Genesis 3:8, RSVCE
3 Genesis 3:19, RSVCE
4 Catechism of the Catholic Church, par. 1140
5 Romans 5:20, RSVCE
6 John 20:22-23
7 Romans 3:23, RSVCE
8 Matthew 10:26
9 Palms 69:5
10 Romans 6:23, RSVCE
11 www.phac-aspc.gc.ca/dca-dea/publications/together_e.html. Original source from *"All Together Now"*, © Her Majesty the Queen in Right of Canada, represented by the Minister of Public Works and Government Services Canada, 1999
12 Catechism of the Catholic Church, par. 1445
13 John 20:22-23, RSVCE
14 Catechism of the Catholic Church, par. 1449
15 Catechism of the Catholic Church, par. 1548
16 1 John 1:9, RSVCE

Chapter 6 – It Can't Get Better

1 Matthew 9:21, RSVCE
2 Luke 8:44-46, NRSV

3 Luke 8:43
4 Luke 8:47-48, NRSV
5 Luke 8:43, NRSV
6 Matthew 5:6, RSVCE
7 John 15:5, RSVCE
8 1 Corinthians 13:1, RSVCE
9 John 6:56, RSVCE
10 Catechism of the Catholic Church, par. 571
11 Catechism of the Catholic Church, par. 654
12 Compendium of the Catechism of the Catholic Church, par. 280
13 Compendium of the Catechism of the Catholic Church, par. 274
14 Compendium of the Catechism of the Catholic Church, par. 271
15 Father Stefano Manelli, *"Jesus Our Eucharistic Love"*, (Niagara Falls, Ontario: St. Monica Publishing), 19
16 John 6:53, RSVCE
17 John 6:55, RSVCE
18 John 6:66
19 Matthew 26:26-28, RSVCE
20 Catechism of the Catholic Church, par. 1325
21 Father Stefano Manelli, *"Jesus Our Eucharistic Love"*, (Niagara Falls, Ontario: St. Monica Publishing), pg 11
22 Catechism of the Catholic Church, par. 1416
23 Father Stefano Manelli, *"Jesus Our Eucharistic Love"*, (Niagara Falls, Ontario: St. Monica Publishing), pg 19

Chapter 7 – A Life Giving Choice

1 Luke 6:37, RSVCE
2 Matthew 6:14, RSVCE
3 Catechism of the Catholic Church, par. 2840
4 Matthew 6:15, RSVCE
5 2 Corinthians 9:6 (RSVCE)
6 Hebrews 12:15, RSVCE
7 Compendium of the Catechism of the Catholic Church, par. 595
8 Galatians 6:7
9 Catechism of the Catholic Church, par. 598
10 Ephesians 4:32, RSVCE
11 Romans 5:20
12 Matthew 6:12, RSVCE
13 Matthew 6:6, RSVCE
14 Matthew 19:26, RSVCE

End Notes (continued)

15 Luke 23:34, RSVCE

16 Pietor DiDoato, *"The Penitent"* (Hawthorne Books, N.Y., 1962), 142. Found at http://credo.stormloader.com/Saints/stgoretti.htm

17 Pietor DiDoato, *"The Penitent"* (Hawthorne Books, N.Y., 1962), 142. Found at http://credo.stormloader.com/Saints/stgoretti.htm

18 Philippians 4:14

Chapter 8 – Living With An Eternal Perspective

1 CCO is a university student movement dedicated to evangelization. For more information on Catholic Christian Outreach, visit www.cco.ca

2 Catechism of the Catholic Church, par. 1021

3 Catechism of the Catholic Church, par 1021

4 Matthew 6:21

5 Matthew 6:20

6 John 14:15

7 Matthew 24:40

8 Found at www.tvturnoff.org/factsheets.htm

9 Catechism of the Catholic Church, par. 1022

10 Father Stefano Manelli, *"Jesus Our Eucharistic Love"*, (Niagara Falls, Ontario: St. Monica Publishing), pg 22

11 Father Stefano Manelli, *"Jesus Our Eucharistic Love"*, (Niagara Falls, Ontario: St. Monica Publishing), pg 22

12 Father Stefano Manelli, *"Jesus Our Eucharistic Love"*, (Niagara Falls, Ontario: St. Monica Publishing), pg. 12

13 Catechism of the Catholic Church, par. 1024

14 Catechism of the Catholic Church, par. 1803

15 Matthew 7:13-14, RSVCE

Chapter 9 – The Catholic Church; God's Idea

1 Found at supersizeme.com

2 Found at supersizeme.com

3 Romans 10:9, RSVCE

4 John 16:13, RSVCE

5 Mark 2:7, RSVCE

6 John 6:63, RSVCE

7 Matthew 16:18, RSVCE

8 Why The Church? By Canon Francis J. Ripley found at www.catholicanswers.com

9 Catechism of the Catholic Church, par. 858

10 Matthew 10:40, RSVCE

11 Matthew 28:20, RSVCE

12 John 16:13

13 Catechism of the Catholic Church, par. 889

14 Matthew 16:19, RSVCE

15 Matthew 28:20

16 Matthew 26:26, RSVCE

17 John 16:13

18 2 Timothy 3:16, RSVCE

19 1 Corinthians 11:2, RSVCE

20 2 Thessalonians 2:15, RSVCE

21 2 Thessalonians 3:6, RSVCE

22 2 Timothy. 2:2, RSVCE

23 1 Corinthians 15:3, RSVCE

24 John 17:20-22, NRSV

25 Luke 10:16, RSVCE

26 Catechism of the Catholic Church, par. 776

27 Compendium of the Catechism of the Catholic Church, par. 162

Chapter 10 – Touching The Wood

1 Luke 23:26, NRSV

2 *"Send Me Your Guardian Angel,"* Padre Pio, 4th Edition, by Fr. Alessio Parente O.F.M. CAP., p.65, (Foggia, 1983).

3 Colossians 1:24, RSVCE

4 Ephesians 3:13, RSVCE

5 1 Peter 4:12-13, RSVCE

6 Catechism of the Catholic Church, par. 1591

7 Romans 12:1, NRSV

8 Luke 22:42, NRSV

9 Romans 8:18, RSVCE

10 Philippians 3:10, RSVCE

11 Found at www.niagarafallslive.com

12 Luke 23:43, RSVCE

13 Luke 23:34, RSVCE

14 John 19:27, RSVCE

15 1 Corinthians 13:7, RSVCE

16 Found at www.quotationspage.com published by Michael and Laura Moncur

17 Romans 8:22-23, NRSV

Chapter 11 – Trials of Faith

1 Genesis 12:1, RSVCE

2 Deuteronomy 31:6, RSVCE

3 John 6:51, RSVCE

4 John 6:52, RSVCE

5 John 6:55, RSVCE

6 John 6:66, RSVCE

7 John 6:67, RSVCE

8 John 6:68-69, RSVCE

9 Hebrew 11:6, RSVCE
10 Matthew 18:3, RSVCE
11 Genesis 3:5-6, RSVCE
12 Psalm 119:105, RSVCE
13 John 11:6
14 John 11:21, 32, RSVCE
15 John 11:33, RSVCE
16 John 11:41-44, NRSV
Chapter 12 – Mary, Our Model of Perfect Surrender

1 Deuteronomy 22:23-24, RSVCE
2 Luke 1:38, RSVCE
3 Catechism of the Catholic Church, par. 494
4 Luke 1:28, RSVCE
5 Luke 1:33
6 Matthew 2:13-14, RSVCE
7 www.sistersofmary.org
8 Matthew 6:33, RSVCE
9 http://www.ewtn.com/therese/therese.htm, taken from *The Story of a Soul,* by St. Therese of Lisieux
10 Luke 1:42, RSVCE
11 http://carmelnet.org/chas/therese.htm, taken from *The Story of a Soul,* by St. Therese of Lisieux
12 Luke 1:32, RSVCE
13 Luke 1:33, RSVCE
14 Matthew 27:46, NRSV
15 Catechism of the Catholic Church, par. 973
16 Luke 1:28, RSVCE
17 Deuteronomy 5:16, RSVCE
18 Compendium of the Catechism of the Catholic Church, par. 973
19 John 19:26-27, RSVCE
20 Compendium of the Catechism of the Catholic Church, par. 100
21 Compendium of the Catechism of the Catholic Church, par. 975

Chapter 13 – The Hinge of Humility

1 Genesis 2:16-17
2 Genesis 3:4-5, RSVCE
3 Genesis 3:1, RSVCE
4 James 4:6, RSVCE
5 Luke 18:16-17, RSVCE
6 2 Corinthians 12:10, RSVCE
7 John 8:32, NRSV
8 Philippians 2:8, NRSV
9 Mother Teresa: *Come Be My Light - The Private*

Writings of the Saint of Calcutta, edited with commentary by Brian Kolodiejchuk, page 285
10 Matthew 26:26, RSVCE
11 John 13:34, NRSV
12 Matthew 20:27, NRSV
13 Matthew 16:16, RSVCE
14 John 13:15. NRSV
15 Matthew 6:1, RSVCE
16 John 12:26, NRSV
17 Revelations 3:20, RSVCE

Chapter 14 – The Encounter of God's Thirst With Ours

1 Catechism of the Catholic Church, par 2744
2 John 17:3, NRSV
3 Catechism of the Catholic Church, par 2744
4 Catechism of the Catholic Church, par 2560
5 Psalm 46:10, RSVCE
6 Catechism of the Catholic Church, par 2700

Fundraiser for One Way Publishing House

A Mile in My Shoes
by Canadian Artist Glen Scrimshaw

Enjoy the captivating and inspiring artwork of highly acclaimed artist, Glen Scrimshaw, in this book "The Stories Behind the Paintings." Each story contains many insights of this unique artist, who often hides little details in his work that add to the intrigue of his artistry.

One Way Publishing House recently published *A Mile in My Shoes* by Glen Scrimshaw. This beautiful coffee table book would make a delightful gift for any art lover and for children to grow in appreciation for art. Because of the value of Glen's internationally renowned artwork, this book retails for $49.95.

When you make a $60 donation to the on-going ministry work of One Way Publishing House, we will send you a copy of this book, shipping and handling included.

Also available in bulk discount!
1-800-705-7396
www.onewaypublishinghouse.com

Fiction for Men and Women of All Ages

Arms of Love and *Surrender*
by Catholic Author Carmen Marcoux
as featured on EWTN

Carmen and James Marcoux and their nine children
September 2010

"Carmen Marcoux's novels about young love, the
challenges of chaste relationships, and the heartaches
and rewards involved in living the Gospel message
without compromise, are simply too good to put down."

Available in bulk discount to help you evangelize with these inspiring novels and the power of fiction!

1-800-705-7396
www.onewaypublishinghouse.com

A New Catholic Series for Children

The Parish Picnic
from the *Tales of Not-So-Long Ago Series*
Hard Cover ~ available November 2010

The Tales of Not-So-Long Ago Series was written by James and Carmen (author of *Arms of Love* and *Surrender*) in collaboration with their family, to inspire young children and their parents to live fully the life of faith. Each book delightfully presents a different Christian virtue in a memorable little tale that takes place in Tuckerville: an endearing, make-belief town "tucked away" in Sunshine Valley.

Rebekah Marcoux's love for art began from the moment she could hold a crayon. Given instruction by her grandmother at an early age, Rebekah's artistic skills flourished. She began selling pencil portrait art by the age of fourteen. At sixteen years old she received her first set of acrylic paints and undertook the task of illustrating the *Tales of Not-So-Long Ago Series*. Rebekah intends to continue a career in art, using her God-given talents to build His Kingdom. She hopes to inspire young people to realize that they are never too young to serve the Lord!

Available in bulk discount!
1-800-705-7396
www.onewaypublishinghouse.com

Place Virtues into Everyone's Hand

Pure Virtue Playing Cards
for all your card playing games

Quality playing cards for hours and hours of great, wholesome fun with family and friends. Playing cards are a fun way to place virtues into everyone's hand! Each card features a different virtue with a passage from Scripture.

"Provide me now a man who can play well,
and bring him to me."
1 Samuel 16:17

Available in bulk discount!
1-800-705-7396
www.onewaypublishinghouse.com